Contents

D1476249

Licence

Text © Pat Hoodless
© 2003 Scholastic Ltd

Published by Scholastic Ltd, Villiers House,
Clarendon Avenue, Leamington Spa,
Warwickshire CV32 5PR

Printed by Bell & Bain Ltd, Glasgow

234567890   3456789012

British Library Cataloguing-in-Publication Data
A catalogue record for this book is available from
the British Library.

ISBN 0-590-53477-7

Visit our website at www.scholastic.co.uk

CD developed in association with
Footmark Media Ltd

Author
Pat Hoodless

Editor
Dulcie Booth

Assistant Editor
Roanne Charles

Series Designer
Joy Monkhouse

Designer
Catherine Mason

Cover photographs
© Photodisc, © Illustrated London
News, © Joy Monkhouse,
© National Railway Musuem/
Science & Society Picture Library

Acknowledgements

Every effort has been made to trace copyright holders and the publishers
apologise for any omissions.

The right of Pat Hoodless to be identified as the author of this work has
been asserted by her in accordance with the Copyright, Designs and Patents
Act 1988.

List of resources on the CD-ROM

The page numbers refer to the teacher's notes provided in this book.

INTRODUCTION

This book and CD-ROM support the teaching and learning set out in the QCA Scheme of Work for history in Year 2. The CD provides a large bank of visual and oral resources. The book provides teacher's notes, background information, ideas for discussion and activities to accompany the CD resources, along with photocopiable pages to support the teaching. All have been specifically chosen to meet the requirements for resources listed in the QCA units 'Why do we remember Florence Nightingale?', 'How do we know about the Great Fire of London' and 'What are we remembering on Remembrance Day?'. The resources are also relevant to those not following the QCA Schemes of Work – the chapter on transport is provided for those following the Scottish curriculum for primary history.

The resources and activities are not intended to be used rigidly, however, since they do not provide a structure for teaching in themselves. The teacher's notes provide ideas for discussion and activities which focus on the 'Knowledge, skills and understanding' of the National Curriculum for history. They aim to guide teachers in developing the children's skills and concepts fundamental to early understanding of what it is to learn about the past. The focus is on developing the children's awareness of similarity and difference, sequencing, understanding chronology, questioning and investigating historical sources and communicating findings in a variety of ways.

Links with other subjects
Literacy
There are a number of close links between the topics covered in this book and literacy. The discussion activities contribute directly to the requirements for speaking and listening. The stories and accounts may be used in shared reading during the Literacy Hour, or to provide a stimulus for shared, guided or independent writing. There is considerable opportunity for the children to develop their independent writing skills in the form of journal entries and letters. Pictures from the CD can be printed to stimulate independent writing or to illustrate it.

Geography
In discussing issues and events throughout this book, geographical links are indispensable. For example, children look at a map of Europe at the time of Crimean War in the chapter on Florence Nightingale, compare images of London when learning about the Great Fire of London and learn about the countries that were involved in the First World War when studying Remembrance Day. The chapter on transport inevitably has a strong geographical focus.

Art and design
There are close links with art and design. Much work at Year 2 needs to be visual. Wherever possible, activities in the teacher's notes make extensive use of it to extend the children's understanding of a particular topic or concept. For example, opportunities for children to make their own card poppies are included in the chapter on Remembrance Day and in the chapter on the Great Fire of London, the children make their own block prints of the fire.

Furthermore, through looking at the portraits, paintings and photographs provided on the CD, children will become naturally involved in discussion of the ideas, methods and techniques used by artists. The resources will also provide opportunities for children to develop their own creativity and understanding of line, shapes and colour. Finally, the resources will help the children to appreciate the different roles and functions of art at different times in the past, particularly the importance of art as a historical source.

Design and technology
Some chapters relate closely to technological developments, in particular 'Transport'.

ICT
Finally, there are clear links with information technology. ICT is constantly useful throughout these activities, particularly in terms of providing an inexhaustible resource for children to use in carrying out research into specific aspects of each topic.

HOW TO USE THE CD-ROM

Windows NT users

If you use Windows NT you may see the following error message: 'The procedure entry point Process32First could not be located in the dynamic link library KERNEL32.dll'. Click on **OK** and the CD will autorun with no further problems.

Setting up your computer for optimal use

On opening, the CD will alert you if changes are needed in order to operate the CD at its optimal use. There are three changes you may be advised to make:

Viewing resources at their maximum screen size

To see images at their maximum screen size, your screen display needs to be set to 800 x 600 pixels. In order to adjust your screen size you will need to **Quit** the program.

If using a PC, open the **Control Panel**. Select **Display** and then **Settings**. Adjust the **Desktop Area** to 800 x 600 pixels. Click on **OK** and then restart the program.

If using a Mac, from the **Apple** menu select **Control Panels** and then **Monitors** to adjust the screen size.

Adobe Acrobat Reader

To print high-quality versions of images and to view and print the photocopiable pages on the CD you need **Adobe Acrobat Reader** installed on your computer. If you do not have it installed already, a version is provided on the CD. To install this version **Quit** the 'Ready Resources' program.

If using a PC, right-click on the **Start** menu on your desktop and choose **Explore**. Click on the + sign to the left of the CD drive entitled 'Ready Resources' and open the folder called 'Acrobat Reader Installer'. Run the program contained in this folder to install **Adobe Acrobat Reader**.

If using a Mac, double click on the 'Ready Resources' icon on the desktop and on the 'Acrobat Reader Installer' folder. Run the program contained in this folder to install **Adobe Acrobat Reader**.

PLEASE NOTE: If you do not have **Adobe Acrobat Reader** installed, you will not be able to print high-quality versions of images, or to view or print photocopiable pages (although these are provided in the accompanying book and can be photocopied).

QuickTime

In order to view the videos and listen to the audio on this CD you will need to have **QuickTime version 5 or later** installed on your computer. If you do not have it installed already, or have an older version of **QuickTime**, the latest version is provided on the CD. If you choose to install this version, **Quit** the 'Ready Resources' program.

If using a PC, right-click on the **Start** menu on your desktop and choose **Explore**. Click on the + sign to the left of the CD drive that is entitled 'Ready Resources' and open the folder called 'QuickTime Installer'. Run the program contained in this folder to install **QuickTime**.

If using a Mac, double click on the 'Ready Resources' CD icon on the desktop and then on the 'Acrobat Reader Installer' folder. Run the program contained in this folder to install **QuickTime**.

PLEASE NOTE: If you do not have **QuickTime** installed you will be unable to view the films.

Menu screen

▶ Click on the **Resource Gallery** of your choice to view the resources available under that topic.
▶ Click on **Complete Resource Gallery** to view all the resources available on the CD.
▶ Click on **Photocopiable Resources (PDF format)** to view a list of the photocopiables provided in the book that accompanies this CD.
▶ **Back**: click to return to the **opening screen**. Click **Continue** to move to the **Menu screen**.
▶ **Quit**: click **Quit** to close the menu program and progress to the **Quit screen.** If you quit from the **Quit screen** you will exit the CD. If you do not quit you will return to the **Menu screen**.

Resource Galleries

▶ **Help**: click **Help** to find support on accessing and using images.
▶ **Back to menu:** click here to return to the **Menu screen**.
▶ **Quit:** click here to move to the **Quit screen** – see **Quit** above.

Viewing images

Small versions of each image are shown in the Resource Gallery. Click and drag the slider on the slide bar to scroll through the images in the Resource Gallery, or click on the arrows to move the images frame by frame. Roll the pointer over an image to see the caption.

▶ Click on an image to view the screen-sized version of it.

▶ To return to the Resource Gallery click on **Back to Resource Gallery**.

Viewing videos

Click on the video icon of your choice in the Resource Gallery. In order to view the videos on this CD, you will need to have **QuickTime** installed on your computer (see 'Setting up your computer for optimal use' above).

Once at the video screen, use the buttons on the bottom of the video screen to operate the video. The slide bar can be used for a fast forward and rewind. To return to the Resource Gallery click on **Back to Resource Gallery**.

Listening to sound recordings

Click on the required sound icon. Use the buttons or the slide bar to hear the sound. A transcript will be displayed on the viewing screen where appropriate. To return to the Resource Gallery, click on **Back to Resource Gallery**.

Printing

Click on the image to view it (see 'Viewing images' above). There are two print options:

Print using Acrobat enables you to print a high-quality version of an image. Choosing this option means that the image will open as a read-only page in **Adobe Acrobat** and in order to access these files you will need to have already installed **Adobe Acrobat Reader** on your computer (see 'Setting up your computer for optimal use' above). To print the selected resource, select **File** and then **Print**. Once you have printed the resource **minimise** or **close** the Adobe screen using — or **X** in the top right-hand corner of the screen. Return to the Resource Gallery by clicking on **Back to Resource Gallery**.

Simple print enables you to print a lower quality version of the image without the need to use **Adobe Acrobat Reader**. Select the image and click on the **Simple print** option. After printing, click on **Back to Resource Gallery**.

Slideshow presentation

If you would like to present a number of resources without having to return to the Resource Gallery and select a new image each time, you can compile a slideshow. Click on the **+** tabs at the top of each image in the Resource Gallery you would like to include in your presentation (pictures, sound and video can be included). It is important that you click on the images in the order in which you would like to view them (a number will appear on each tab to confirm the order). If you would like to change the order, click on **Clear slideshow** and begin again. Once you have selected your images – up to a maximum of 20 – click on **Play slideshow** and you will be presented with the first of your selected resources. To move to the next selection in your slideshow click on **Next slide**, to see a previous resource click on **Previous slide**. You can end your slideshow presentation at any time by clicking on **Resource Gallery**. Your slideshow selection will remain selected until you **Clear slideshow** or return to the **Menu screen**.

Viewing on an interactive whiteboard or data projector

Resources can be viewed directly from the CD. To make viewing easier for a whole class, use a large monitor, data projector or interactive whiteboard. For group, paired or individual work, the resources can be viewed from the computer screen.

Photocopiable resources (PDF format)

To view or print a photocopiable resource page, click on the required title in the list and the page will open as a read-only page in **Adobe Acrobat**. In order to access these files you will need to have already installed **Adobe Acrobat Reader** on your computer (see 'Setting up your computer for optimal use' above). To print the selected resource select **File** and then **Print**. Once you have printed the resource **minimise** or **close** the Adobe screen using — or **X** in the top right-hand corner of the screen. This will take you back to the list of PDF files. To return to the **Menu screen**, click on **Back**.

FLORENCE NIGHTINGALE

Content, skills and concepts

This chapter relates to unit 4 in the QCA Scheme of Work for history at Key Stage 1, 'Why do we remember Florence Nightingale?', and can be used to assist teachers in planning, resourcing and meeting the objectives of the unit. Together with the Florence Nightingale Resource Gallery on the CD-ROM, it introduces a range of mainly visual sources that focus on this significant person from a time beyond living memory. It also looks at the background to her work – the Crimean War – and provides material to support the teaching of similarities and differences between nursing today and in the past.

At Year 1, children will already have gained experience in sequencing, using time-related vocabulary, and using pictures and written sources. Recounting parts of stories about the past, and comparing past and present are other activities that will have introduced the relevant skills and concepts needed in order to progress to this unit. Suggestions for the further development of these skills form part of this chapter.

Resources on the CD-ROM

A map of Europe at the time of the Crimean War and pictures of Florence herself, of Queen Victoria, of a battlefield and of nurses and hospitals in the past and the present are provided on the CD. Teacher's notes containing background information about these sources are included in this chapter, along with ideas for activities. Also on the CD is a sound recording of Florence speaking. This recording provides the children with first-hand experience of a Victorian person speaking.

Photocopiables pages

Photocopiable resources can be found within the book and are also provided in PDF format on the CD-ROM from which they can be printed. They include:
▶ a timeline
▶ word cards which highlight the essential vocabulary of this topic
▶ the story of Florence Nightingale's life
▶ an extract from a soldier's journal at the time of the Crimean War.
The teacher's notes that accompany the photocopiable pages include suggestions for ways of using the pages for whole class, group or individual activities.

History skills

Skills such as observing, describing, using time-related vocabulary, sequencing, using a timeline, comparing, inferring, listening, speaking, reading, writing and drawing are all involved in the activities suggested, for both the resources on the CD and the photocopiable pages. For example, there is an opportunity to develop sequencing skills through the use of the timeline of Florence Nightingale's life, which is on a small enough scale for children to comprehend. Children can learn to use descriptive vocabulary to describe the pictures of battle scenes and hospitals. They will listen to a recording and make recordings of events in their own lives. They will also write their own newspaper articles, diary entries and letters.

Historical understanding

In the course of the suggested tasks, a further aim is for children to begin to develop a more detailed knowledge of the past and to sequence events independently, through their understanding of the context and content of the factual information they use. They will begin to give reasons for Florence Nightingale's actions, use sources to find further information about her and be able to recount her life story. They will also develop an awareness that in some ways things are different in the past, but in other ways the same. Some of the more formal vocabulary related to history and chronology, such as *Victorian*, is introduced in this chapter.

Photograph © Ingram Publishing

NOTES ON THE CD-ROM RESOURCES

Map of Europe at the time of the Crimean War

This outline map shows Europe with some of the major states and kingdoms labelled. However, the political organisation of the Italian and German kingdoms is so complex at this time, the map only shows those nations engaged in the Crimean War, that is Britain, France, the Ottoman Empire (Turkish) and the opposing nation of Russia. The war had broken out because Russia had been taking land from the Turkish rulers of the Ottoman Empire, in an attempt to acquire a way through to the Black Sea. This, of course would have been important to all involved because of its strategic significance. The Turks, French and British feared that it would be an important step towards Russian expansion into their sphere of influence.

Scutari is shown so that the children can, if wished, try to work out and research the route that Florence and her team of nurses took. They travelled on ships going from port to port, and the journey will have been quite a long and arduous one.

Discussing the map
▶ Show the children the map and discuss the time in the past that it shows. Point out how it shows different countries at the time of the Crimean War (1854–6). Discuss the reasons for the war.
▶ Find volunteers to read the names of the places shown. Ask which places the children think are *countries* and which they think are *towns*. Discuss the difference between these, giving examples from your local area as comparisons.
▶ See if anyone can find the Crimea. Ask them to point out Scutari.
▶ Can any of the children work out a sea route from England to the Crimea? How would Florence have travelled there? (By sea, via Marseilles and through the Mediterranean.)
▶ Look at the position of Scutari. Discuss how far away it is from the Crimea. How would the wounded soldiers have been taken there, and how long might it have taken? (In bad weather, the wounded were kept for days waiting for an opportunity to sail, near Balaclava, a port in the south, which became very crowded.)

Activities
▶ Give the children copies of the map to colour the seas and countries in different colours. Make the countries on one side in the war one colour and the other a second colour. Remind the children that Russia was on one side and Britain, France and Turkey were on the other.
▶ Discuss the reasons for the war. They were fighting over the Crimea, which Russia wanted to take away from the Turkish Empire.
▶ Help the children find the right place for the war on a general class timeline. Add a label to it to mark the war.
▶ Ask if the children know the names of any other countries on the map and help them to label them.
▶ Discuss how maps can change. Explain that borders and boundaries can change after wars, when a country might win and take some land from their enemy. Maps made before this happen then become historical maps, because they are now showing what things were like in the past. This map, therefore, is a historical map. Ask the children to look at the same area in a modern atlas.

Portrait of Florence Nightingale

Florence Nightingale was born on 12 May 1820. When the Crimean War broke out, she was 34 years old. She had already spent much of her adult life working as a nurse, sometimes against the wishes of her parents. In this portrait, she will have been in her late thirties just after the war ended. She looks quite serious, in keeping with her very religious outlook on life and her belief that she had been called by God to do his will. Florence's family were not especially wealthy, but were comfortably enough off that her father did not need to earn a living. This is borne out by the subdued, but very well-made and well-designed clothes Florence is wearing. Her hairstyle is in a typical Victorian style, and adorned with a lace cap. She has jewellery and lovely lace details, such as on the collar of her dress. In this picture, she looks quite young, but sombre, after she has worked in the horrors of war, perhaps.

Discussing the portrait

▶ Tell the children that this is a picture of Florence Nightingale, a famous nurse who looked after wounded soldiers in Victorian times.

▶ Find the dates of her birth and death on the class timeline and help the children put labels in the right place.

▶ Ask what kind of picture the children think this is, for example a portrait or photograph.

▶ Ask for volunteers to guess what age Florence was when this portrait was drawn. Challenge the children to work out how long ago it was drawn.

▶ Talk about the details of her dress. Why does it look old-fashioned? How is it different from modern dress?

Activities

▶ Ask the children if they think Florence looks like a rich person or a poor person. Discuss reasons for their decision, for example her clothes, her neatness, the fact that she had her portrait drawn.

▶ What sort of person do the children think she was from looking at the portrait? What is the evidence for this? Work with the class to make a list of words, describing Florence's character as it appears in the portrait.

▶ Provide pairs of children with sketching materials to make portraits of each other.

▶ Read with the children the story of Florence's life on photocopiable pages 22–3.

Portrait of Queen Victoria

Here, Queen Victoria is in her late thirties. Albert, her husband, has not yet died, and she is dressed in her full, highly colourful royal regalia. A typical feature of Victoria's portraits was the small crown and train which she liked to wear. Coming to the throne following a period in which the monarchy were extremely unpopular, Victoria made every effort to regain public respect. She emphasised family values, took her role as monarch very seriously, and dressed for the part. The photograph provides a useful opportunity for young children to begin to notice features of the way the monarch dressed, and some parts of the royal regalia evident here, such as the medals and the royal sash.

Discussing the photograph

▶ Ask the children if they can guess who is in this picture. If they do not realise it, explain that Queen Victoria was the monarch at the time of the Crimean War.

▶ Do they think it is a painting or a photograph? Why is this?

▶ How is the Queen made to look important? For example, the special chair (maybe a throne), her dress and regalia.

▶ Discuss the details of her dress. What makes it look very rich?

▶ Does she wear anything else as well as her rich dress? Ask volunteers to point out the extra things she wears. Discuss the names of these, for example *crown*, *sash*, *medals*, *necklace*, *earrings*, *rings*, *bracelet*, *lace cap and train*, *brooch*.

▶ Discuss why the Queen might have had her photograph taken. (Queen Victoria was a big fan of photography as a new technology so was keen to use it where possible.) Link this idea to the great inventions of the Victorian age and challenge the children to make a list of the great inventions they can discover.

▶ How does the Queen look – happy, serious, stern, and so on? Discuss which words best describe her expression and pose.

Activities

▶ Place the dates of Victoria's birth, coronation and death on the class timeline. Show the children the sequence of events and the *span* of time we now call *Victorian* because of Queen Victoria's reign.

▶ Find other pictures of Queen Victoria, showing her both younger and older. Notice how she suddenly began to wear black clothes and explain that this was what she did when her husband Albert died in 1861. She only ever wore black from that time.

▶ Find out about Victoria's life and make a list of the key events. During a shared writing session, make a timeline of Victoria's life for the children to put into their topic books on Florence Nightingale.

▶ Show a suitable extract from a documentary or film about Victoria, such as *Mrs Brown*.

Battle of Balaclava, 1854

The full horror of warfare in the 19th century is captured in this picture. A particular disaster occurred during the Crimean War when a brigade of British troops, the Light Brigade, was ordered to charge into a very dangerous valley, where they were at great risk of being ambushed. In the ensuing chaos, many British soldiers lost their lives.

Although the painting may have been produced to commemorate the tragedy of the charge of the Light Brigade, and may be a little exaggerated, it does show what kind of fighting took place. Infantrymen had to fight hand to hand, with bayonets and swords. The officers used pistols at close range and could also wield swords from their greater height on horseback. The whole event would have been noisy, bloody and terrifying.

The picture will be useful in stimulating children to make comments and describe what they think it must have been like to be a soldier in the Crimean War.

Discussing the picture

▶ Ask the children what they think is happening in this picture. Tell them about the Crimean War and place the dates of the war (1854–6) on the class timeline.

▶ Explain that this is a picture of a famous event that took place in the Crimean War, called 'The Charge of the Light Brigade'. Explain briefly what happened: the British troops were ordered to charge against a much more powerful force (the Russians); they were trapped and were nearly all killed. It was the worst defeat of the war.

▶ Get the children to look very closely at the picture. Ask what weapons they can see.

▶ Again looking closely, ask if they can see soldiers from Britain or soldiers from Russia. Is it clear which side they are on? Direct them to clues such as the square fur hats that are worn by the Russian troops. Ask if the children can tell which side is winning.

▶ Ask the children what impression the picture gives, for example chaos and confusion. Discuss how this is probably what the artist wanted to show.

▶ Discuss with the children what they think it must have been like in such a battle. What do they think happened to most of the British soldiers?

Activities

▶ Look at the 'Map of Europe at the time of the Crimean War' (provided on the CD) and remind the children which countries were fighting.

▶ Make a wall display of pictures of the important people at the time of the Crimean War and the battles that took place.

▶ Provide the children with appropriate books and accounts and ask them to try to find out more about the war. What happened to the soldiers when they were ill or hurt?

▶ Read to the children the beginning of Tennyson's 'The Charge of the Light Brigade', provided on photocopiable page 25.

▶ Use the newspaper report on photocopiable page 24 to find out how the wounded soldiers were cared for.

▶ Make a large wall collage, showing battles like this, for example the Battle of Sebastopol (or others fought in this way, with horses and a lot of hand-to-hand fighting).

Hospital at Scutari

This painting shows a ward inside the military hospital at Scutari. Florence Nightingale can be seen, looking very efficient, discussing some papers with an officer. It is clear that by this time the effects of Florence's policies are in evidence. The ward is clean and the patients look comfortable in well-made beds. There is clean linen on the beds and nurses are available to help patients move around and eat. Comfortable mattresses are available, as can be seen from the empty bed, along with sufficient pillows and blankets.

During the first winter after Florence's arrival at Scutari, soldiers were suffering badly from the cold of the winter (of similar severity to that in Russia) and many were even freezing to death because of the lack of adequate provisions. It is noticeable that a heater has been placed in the ward, where soldiers recovering from their wounds could sit to talk while keeping warm. They have also been provided with clean gowns and shoes to wear while in the hospital. Proper ventilation has been provided with open windows, and the flue from the stove taking the smoke and fumes outside. The ward appears very light and airy and the needs of the patients appear to be being met.

Discussing the painting

▶ Prior to looking at this picture, it will be useful to have talked about the dreadful conditions in hospitals at this time, both military and ordinary ones. Describe the conditions to the class, for example dirty, cold, draughty, no nurses, no proper food, patients lying on floors, rats and so on.

▶ Ask the children what they can see in this picture. Who can they see in it? For example, Florence, an officer, a nurse, patients.

▶ Ask volunteers to describe the ward. What does it look like? Ask why the ward looked like this. Explain how Florence had worked to achieve this.

▶ Briefly tell the children the story of Florence's life if they have not heard it before – see photocopiable pages 22–3. Explain how she believed she was called by God to do this caring work.

▶ Look back at the painting and ask the children to discuss what they think Florence has achieved, for example more nurses and helpers, food, clean beds and clothes, warm heaters, and so on.

Activities

▶ Look for Scutari on the 'Map of Europe at the time of the Crimean War' (provided on the CD).

▶ Make a list of words to describe the military hospital before Florence arrived, and then a list to describe it when she had been working there.

▶ During a shared writing session, compose a paragraph about what Florence had achieved at the hospital at Scutari.

▶ Find more information and pictures about hospitals in the first part of Queen Victoria's reign. Provide children with the opportunity to put copies of pictures in their topic books and to draw some of their own.

▶ Compare the picture of the ward at Scutari with the photograph of the 'Modern ward', provided on the CD (see the notes on page 12).

▶ As part of a drama lesson, show the children how to make a 'freeze-frame' of a battle scene or of a hospital scene at the time of the war.

▶ Listen to the sound recording 'Florence Nightingale speaking', provided on the CD. Ask the children if this gives us any clues as to what Florence thinks she achieved.

The Lady with the Lamp

It is from sketches like these that the popular name for Florence Nightingale arose. Here she is inspecting the wards at night, carrying a small lamp. From the stories told and these pictures, she soon came to be known as 'the Lady with the Lamp'. She is said to have given much sympathy, support and hope to many wounded and dying soldiers. These men fully appreciated the care that Florence and her nurses gave them, although recent research suggests that the actual medical treatment she gave did not produce the improvements reported at the time. Florence had worked hard to achieve even this, in the face of strong opposition from senior members of the medical profession and army officials, who were convinced that it was unsuitable for female nurses to work in military hospitals. However, the situation in the Crimea became so bad, with so many men dying from neglect, that these men soon had to allow Florence and her team of nurses to work on the wards.

Discussing the picture

▶ Ask the children what they think this picture shows. Who can they see? Where is she? What do they think she is doing?

▶ Why do they think Florence is going round at night with a lamp? Why should she do this? (For example, she wanted to be sure that her patients were cared for during the night and took a lamp so that she would be able to see if all was well.) Emphasise to the children that there would have been no electricity at this time.

▶ Ask the children to look closely at Florence and comment on the way she is dressed. Does she look like a nurse? Why not?

▶ Ask the children what they think the soldiers thought about Florence.

▶ What kind of person do the children think Florence was? Encourage them to use adjectives, such as *kind*, *caring* and so on.

▶ How would they have liked to have been a patient in a hospital like this?

Activities

▶ Ask the children to find more detail about the life of Florence Nightingale and make a collection of books about her life and the Crimean War.

▶ Encourage the children to collect quotations about Florence Nightingale and make a wall display of these, around a large portrait of her.

▶ Read the story of Mary Seacole to the class and talk about how she was another famous nurse who also worked in the Crimean War. Ask the children to find out more about Mary Seacole and compare her activities with those of Florence Nightingale.

▶ Compare the image of Florence with the photograph of the 'Modern nurse', provided on the CD. How are the clothes of Florence and the modern nurse different? What is different about the nursing equipment they have?

▶ Together with the class, write a short drama scene about Florence Nightingale helping wounded soldiers at Scutari. Provide time for the children to act out the scene.

Modern nurse

This photograph of a present-day nurse provides an opportunity to compare earlier nurses with modern ones. Here we can see major changes in the dress of the nurse since Florence Nightingale's time. This nurse wears a special, recognisable uniform. She still has to ensure her appearance is smart and efficient to inspire trust and respect in her patients. She has some items of equipment attached to her uniform, such as her watch, which she uses when taking blood pressures or temperature readings. She also carries pens and pencils for making notes about her patients as she does her routine checks. She wears an identity card for security purposes, a necessity in the large public hospitals of today.

Discussing the photograph

▶ Ask the children if they think this is a photograph of a nurse today, or at the time of the Crimean War. Discuss how they know.

▶ Ask if any of the children have visited a hospital or have stayed in one.

▶ Ask what we call someone who is ill in hospital.

▶ How many of the children have seen a nurse like this one?

▶ Find volunteers to list the things that this nurse is wearing. Discuss why she has these things as part of her uniform. Why do they think that modern nurses wear uniforms?

Activities

▶ Encourage the children to look at the similarities and differences between this photograph of a modern nurse and the image of Florence Nightingale in 'The Lady with the Lamp' picture, provided on the CD. Let the children work in pairs to work on a list of things that are the same about nurses and things that have changed.

▶ Reinforce what we mean by *change*. Talk about why things change over time.

▶ Together, label a printout of the photograph of the 'Modern nurse' to highlight all the aspects of her uniform and equipment.

▶ Look at the photographs of the 'Modern ward' and the 'Operating theatre', provided on the CD. Provide books and other resources about nursing and hospitals and set the children the task of finding out about the various jobs that nurses do.

▶ Set up a 'hospital' corner as a structured play area. This could change from a modern one to an old-fashioned, 'Victorian' hospital.

Modern ward

This photograph of a modern hospital ward is useful for making comparisons with the ward illustrated in 'Hospital at Scutari' (see page 10). The ward is very clean, with polished floors and clean, tidy beds. There is comfortable bedding for the patients, such as clean sheets, blankets, mattresses and pillows. The patients also have other equipment to help them manage with their disabilities and to make their time in hospital as comfortable as possible. There are specially designed tables for them to use in bed. There are armchairs, charts showing the patients' medical progress, reading lamps and specially designed equipment. This ward also has curtaining, which is used to provide patients with privacy when required. What is particularly noticeable is the large number of nurses available on the ward, looking after the patients and serving their meals.

Discussing the photograph

▶ Ask if the children recognise the scene in this photograph.

▶ Encourage them to look closely at the photograph and talk about the details they observe. Model appropriate vocabulary for them to use, such as *modern*, *ward*, *equipment*.

▶ Talk about the people they can see. Discuss what they are doing.

▶ Ask if any of the children have been in hospital wards like this one, or if they have seen other sorts of wards.

▶ Did any of the children who have been in hospital enjoy their stay? Ask the children if they think the soldiers at the Crimea enjoyed being in hospital.

Activities

▶ Help the class to place this hospital picture, or an appropriate label, on the class timeline. Look back along the timeline at how long ago Florence Nightingale was working in the hospital at Scutari.

▶ Provide the children with the time and hospital word cards (see photocopiable pages 18 and 20) to use when describing the photograph of the modern ward. Challenge more able children to write sentences about the ward scene using the word cards as well as topic-specific vocabulary of their own.

▶ Compare this photograph and the painting of 'Hospital at Scutari'. Focus on both the similarities and differences. Work with the children to identify the changes that have taken place on hospital wards since Victorian times.

▶ Set up a structured play area where the children can play at admitting each other into hospital. Make appointment cards and record sheets for them to fill in about their patients.

Operating theatre

Whereas during the Crimean War treatment for serious injuries would have been carried out in the mud of the battlefield, here we see part of a specially designed operating theatre in a modern hospital. A feature of this photograph is the large amount of equipment used in a modern operation. Much of this equipment is electrical and relies on highly developed technology.

Everything in a modern operation has to be sterile. Serious problems with infections over a long period of time made people realise the importance of keeping an operating theatre and its equipment completely clean and sterile. There is therefore hardly any furniture in the room. The only things are those which are essential for the operation. Small items are kept packed away in airtight packages until they are needed, and there are special ventilating systems to maintain a clean flow of air. Large, strong lights can be lowered from the ceiling. Everyone who goes into the operating theatre must wear special clothing and make sure that their hands are very clean.

Discussing the photograph

▶ Can any of the children explain to the rest of the class what is shown in this photograph?

▶ Discuss why it is called an 'operating theatre', and what it is for.

▶ Look closely at the picture and find volunteers to point out things they recognise. Explain what the other equipment is, where you can.

▶ Discuss why the operating theatre seems so bare.

▶ Talk about sterility and germs, and how doctors and nurses must wash their hands and wear special gloves and gowns when they work here.

▶ Ask if the children have seen a picture of an operating theatre at the hospital in Scutari. Do they think there was one? Where do they think the doctors in the Crimea carried out their surgery? Why was this?

Activities

▶ Find out if anyone in the class has had an operation. If appropriate, find out what they can remember about the experience of being in hospital.

▶ If possible, invite a nurse into the school to talk about their work and about times when he or she has worked in an operating theatre.

▶ Make a list of the modern kinds of equipment available in an operating theatre.

▶ Ask the children to search for other pictures of operating theatres and to write short notes about the things they can see in their pictures.

Florence Nightingale speaking

This is a cylinder recording (lasting about 52 seconds) of Florence Nightingale herself speaking. It was made in 1890 when Florence was 70 years old, so that there would be a record of her voice for posterity. The recording hisses and crackles considerably, but it is still possible to make out what Florence is saying. Her voice sounds strong and clear. She has a very 'Victorian' manner of speaking, and her accent sounds quite aristocratic to us today. The recording is most interesting in the light that it throws upon her own view of her work. She certainly seems to consider it as having been very great work, and seems extremely proud of her achievements. The cylinder, the first machine to record sound and play it back and also known as the phonograph, was invented by Thomas Edison in 1877 and is one example of many important inventions from the Victorian period.

Play the recording to the children. They will find it difficult to make out and very strange at first. The transcript is displayed on the CD as the recording is played (and also provided below). Read the transcript of the recording to them, and you may wish to create and display an enlarged version of it for them to follow. Play the recording a second time, again following the words on the transcript. Finally, play the recording a third time for the children to listen to without the transcript being visible. By this stage, many of them will be able to make out what Florence is saying. However, play the recording again if the children are having problems.

Transcript:
'At Florence Nightingale's house, London. July the 30th. Eighteen hundred and ninety. When I am no longer even a memory, just a name, I hope my voice may perpetuate the great work of my life. God bless my dear old Comrades at Balaclava and bring them safe to shore.'

Discussing the sound recording
▶ Discuss the sound of the recording. Ask the class why they think it sounds like this.
▶ Explain how the recording was made, using a very early technique where the sound was recorded on a cylinder.
▶ Do they think Florence sounds like a young woman?
▶ Encourage the children to think about what Florence is saying. Look at the transcript again. Discuss what she means when she says 'no longer even a memory, just a name'. Ask the children if they think she has achieved what she wanted.
▶ What do they think she means by her 'great work'?
▶ Who do they think Florence is referring to when she talks about her 'dear old Comrades at Balaclava'?

Activities
▶ Ask what we use today to record people's voices and music. (For example, tape recorders.) Play a modern CD and then listen to the recording again. Compare the quality of the sound. Explain that although the recording of Florence is being played from a CD it is not comparable to modern CDs. Tell the children that it was recorded on different equipment (a cylinder) and has been copied onto a modern CD.
▶ Find pictures of early recording devices to share with the class or for a wall display.
▶ Point out how Florence seems proud of her work. Ask the children to find the words in the transcript that tell us this.
▶ Set up a recording area, where the children can make recordings of their own voices talking briefly about the things they have done and what they are particularly proud of. Ask them also to say what they would like to do in the future and what they would like to be remembered for.

NOTES ON THE PHOTOCOPIABLE PAGES

Word cards

A number of specific types of vocabulary have been introduced on the word cards:
▶ words related to the passing of time and chronology, such as *a very long time ago*, *Victorian*
▶ words associated with the Crimean war, such as *soldier*, *Scutari*
▶ words associated with hospitals, such as *nurse*, *ward*.
Encourage the children to think of other appropriate words to add to these, in order to build up a word bank for the theme of Florence Nightingale. They could also use the cards in displays, in matching activities and to help them in writing captions for their pictures. Once you have made copies of the word cards, cut them out and laminate them. Use them as often as possible when talking about Florence Nightingale or for word games.

Activities

▶ Make displays of images of hospitals at different times in the past and in the present and ask the children to label them with the time word cards, for example *modern*, *old-fashioned* and the 'Hospital word cards', for example *nurse*, *patient*.
▶ Begin to encourage the children, during whole class lessons, to think of sentences containing the key words they have learned.
▶ Give the children copies of 'Map of Europe at the time of the Crimean War', with the place names covered and ask them to label the map with the 'Crimean word cards' from photocopiable page 19.

Florence Nightingale timeline

This timeline showing key events in the life of Florence Nightingale can be used to introduce children to the notion of chronology over a person's lifetime. It introduces the idea of a sequence of events presented in chronological order, as well as a small number of significant dates. It could be used alongside 'Portrait of Florence Nightingale' (provided on the CD) and in conjunction with the story of her life (see photocopiable pages 22–3), to give children some visual representation of the sequence of key events in her life. It could be adapted for use in the form of a long string stretched across the classroom, to represent the distance in time covered during her life span. Pictures could be added to show other significant events as the topic progresses. The kind of timeline shown here can also be useful at the end of the topic, for checking children's success in grasping ideas of sequence, chronology and, for those at that stage, understanding of the use of dates.

Discussing the timeline

▶ At the beginning of the topic, ask the class what they think this timeline shows.
▶ Discuss what the numbers on the timeline mean.
▶ Look at the 'reading direction' of the timeline. Show how the numbers are bigger as you read along. Explain that this means time is passing.
▶ Add more dates to the line, such as the decades and get the class to count along the line in tens. Show how a timeline can be rather like a number line, but it means more than a simple line of numbers. Explain how it represents the passing of years.

Activities

▶ Make a class timeline using this as an example. Ask children to place any other pictures or portraits of Florence they find in the appropriate places on the timeline – including 'The Lady with the Lamp' (provided on the CD).
▶ Ask the children to read out the dates and practise saying them correctly. Remind them of the current year and how we say this as a date. See if they can tell you some other dates from the past.
▶ Challenge very able children to work out how old Florence was when certain things happened, and how old she was when she died.
▶ Give the children a timeline with either relevant dates or words and ask them to draw pictures of Florence, or paste on pictures of Florence at these different times. They can use pictures they have found as well as those provided on the CD.

Story of Florence Nightingale

This account tells some of the main events in Florence Nightingale's life. It aims to show the children why Florence wanted to work with the sick and with wounded soldiers, and how that interest arose. It suggests possible religious reasons, but does not emphasis this point for such a young audience. The story aims to show some of the problems she faced, both at home where her parents did not want her to work as a nurse, and in the Crimea, where she was not accepted by the army and those in charge of the hospitals. It outlines her achievements following the Crimean War, her relationship with Queen Victoria, and the invalidity she suffered later in life, possibly because of the nature of her work in nursing. Finally, it suggests why it is that we still remember her.

The story is probably best read to the children as part of a shared reading session, going through any of the unfamiliar vocabulary such as *better-off* and *Commission of Inquiry*. One way of reading the story with the class is to set up a slide show (see page 4) using the following resources from the CD: 'Battle of Balaclava, 1854', 'Hospital at Scutari', 'The Lady with the Lamp' and 'Portrait of Florence Nightingale'. Read the text in conjunction with the slide show as well as the timeline of her life.

Discussing the story
▶ Who can remember from the story how long ago Florence was born?
▶ Discuss why her parents gave her the name Florence.
▶ Ask the children why Florence got angry with people on account of the poor cottagers she had seen.
▶ Why do the children think that Florence's parents did not want her to become a nurse?
▶ What kind of family did she come from? What were her parents probably like?
▶ Why do the children think that Florence worked so hard that she became an invalid?
▶ Why do they think the Queen wanted to meet her?
▶ How is it that today we still know about what Florence did, nearly 200 years later?

Activities
▶ Ask the children to talk about the important things Florence Nightingale did, or to recount the story in their own words. The more able writers, with support, could write their own story of Florence.
▶ Ask for volunteers to find in the story all the things that they can see on the timeline from photocopiable page 21. Ask the children if they can add any more important events to the timeline.
▶ Ask the children to write a letter from Florence Nightingale to her parents upon her arrival in the Crimea. Start them off with the first few sentences, for example *How is everyone at home? I am writing to tell you... I can do much good by...*
▶ Compare Florence's work with that of other famous nurses, such as Mary Seacole, or with famous doctors, like Dr Albert Schweitzer, known for his pioneering medical work in Africa.
▶ Ask the children to find out about Mother Teresa.
▶ Make small topic booklets for the children to complete with their work about Florence Nightingale.
▶ As an extension activity for the very able children, suggest they write an imaginary story about the work of a nurse in the future.

A foot soldier's journal

This extract, rewritten from an actual journal by Charles Usherwood, enables children to imagine what the Crimean War was like from the perspective of an ordinary foot soldier. These soldiers were given orders which they had to obey, although they must have realised the stupidity of leaving behind their kit, food and the tents. The extract shows some of the effects that orders and mistakes like these had on the British army during this war. It could be linked with work on the Charge of the Light Brigade (see the poem on photocopiable page 25 and the picture provided on the CD), another example of terrible mistakes being made which resulted in the deaths of hundreds of people.

This text is probably best read to the children or shared with them during a whole class shared reading session during the Literacy Hour. It is important that the children have time to discuss the context of the journal extract, since it begins after the soldiers have travelled overland across Europe, and then across the Black Sea. They are just disembarking in the Crimea. The text can also be enlarged and read with the children to enable them to point out words or phrases that they find difficult to understand. It will be useful as a stimulus for discussion and for the children's own journal writing.

Discussing the text

▶ After reading the first journal entry, discuss with the class what is happening, where the soldiers are and why they have been on board a ship.

▶ Read on and ask them to pick out phrases which they think sound old-fashioned, for example *rain coming down smartly*. Talk about how things change in time, even the way ordinary people speak and write.

▶ Discuss with the children how they think it was that the soldiers suddenly began to get ill with cholera. Explain that cholera was very contagious and difficult to treat, and that it was already a problem in England too at this time. There had been *epidemics*.

▶ Tell the children that the journal extract is an *eyewitness account*, and discuss what these words mean.

Activities

▶ Find out, or ask the more able children to find out, further details about the course of the Crimean War. Make a timeline of the key events, including the Charge of the Light Brigade.

▶ Provide an outline structure for children to complete their own journal extracts for different events in the war.

▶ Create a short drama about an event in the Crimean War and provide time for children to act this out in groups.

The Charge of the Light Brigade PAGE 25

Alfred Lord Tennyson wrote this poem in 1854 in an attempt to memorialise the tragedy of the Charge of the Light Brigade (see page 10 for more information). Tennyson had been made Poet Laureate by Queen Victoria in 1850 and he became the best-known poet in Victorian England. The poem captured the public mood of the time in its success at portraying both the bravery of the soldiers and the futility and stupidity of the order to charge. Tennyson died in 1892 and many of the survivors of the Battle of Balaclave turned out for his funeral at Westminster Abbey.

The poem is a challenging read and only the first three verses of the poem are provided here. It can be used in conjunction with the painting 'Battle of Balaclava, 1854' (provided on the CD).

Discussing the poem

▶ Read the extract to the children, explaining any unfamiliar vocabulary such as *league, dismay'd, blunder'd*.

▶ Ask the children who or what they think *the six hundred* are. Who do they think is referred to as *he*?

▶ Discuss the situation the soldiers were in. Talk about how they were obliged to follow orders when in a war. Relate this discussion to the lines, *Theirs not to make reply... but to do and die*. Ask for volunteers to say these lines in their own words, for example *They were not allowed to say anything back to the officers*.

▶ Ask the children to picture the scene described in the lines *Cannon to right... thunder'd* and again to explain the situation in their own words.

▶ Discuss why the valley is called *jaws of Death* and *mouth of Hell*.

Activities

▶ During a shared reading session, organise the children to read the poem together as a class. After the reading, set small groups the task of finding rhymes, rhythm, unusual words and so on.

▶ Challenge the children, working in pairs, to write their own rhyming couplets about the Charge of the Light Brigade.

▶ Create a mime, using half the class as the Light Brigade, and the other half as those in ambush with their cannon. At the end of the mime, when nearly all are dead, and all is silent, read the three verses of the poem on the photocopiable page.

a very long time ago

old-fashioned

Victorian

before

after

when

century

modern

Crimean War word cards

soldier
war
Scutari
Russia
Britain
France
Turkish Empire
Crimea

Hospital word cards

nurse
doctor
ward
hygiene
disease
germs
wounds
patient

From left to right, by kind permission of Illustrated London News and © Beverly Curl.

Florence Nightingale timeline

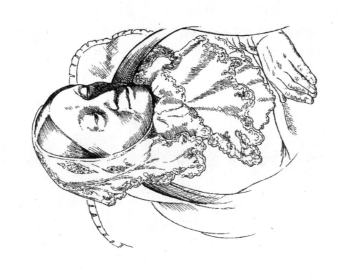

Florence is born
1820

Florence goes to Scutari
1854

Florence dies
1910

Story of Florence Nightingale

We still remember Florence Nightingale although she was born nearly two hundred years ago. Florence was born in 1820, in the Italian town of Florence and her British parents decided to name her after it. She had a happy childhood and grew up in a comfortable home with large gardens in Derbyshire. She always loved caring for animals as a child and as she grew older, she began to be concerned about the poor people living in nearby cottages. She sometimes visited the cottagers with her mother, and became shocked to find that they often could not afford enough to eat, to wear or to keep their homes warm. Florence grew angry that better-off people did not seem to do anything to help the poor. She believed that God wanted her to do something about it. She began to study and work as a nurse.

Her parents did not want Florence to become a nurse. They thought it was not suitable for a young lady. After several years, however, Florence was asked to take a team of nurses to look after the soldiers wounded in a war that was going on at the time. She set off in 1854, with a party of 37 nurses, to travel to the Crimea and work in the military hospitals there. The main military hospital was at Scutari, and this is where Florence first arrived. She was upset at what she saw. There was no water, and no proper beds or wards, just long, dirty halls. The wind whistled down the corridors, rats ran everywhere and the rain ran in through the leaking roof. Florence and her nurses felt powerless to do anything at first because the doctors and officials ignored and distrusted her. They thought she was just a 'society lady' who would not know what to do. They also disapproved of women working as nurses in army hospitals.

As the crisis grew worse, the officials realised that Florence knew what to do and could help them. Finally, they asked her advice and she was able to start work. Florence and her nurses scrubbed the floors, made beds for the soldiers, and went shopping to buy food, clothing and medical equipment. She also bought pillows, mattresses and blankets for the soldiers' beds. When soldiers arrived at the hospital, they would be greeted by Florence. She made sure they had baths, clean clothes, had their wounds dressed and received some food. Some soldiers said it was like heaven after the horrors they had been through.

■SCHOLASTIC
PHOTOCOPIABLE

Story of Florence Nightingale (cont)

At night, Florence went round all the wards with her lamp to check that everyone was safe and comfortable. This is why she came to be called 'The Lady with the Lamp'. William Russell, a reporter for *The Times* newspaper sent back photographs and reports about the terrible conditions at the Crimea. He said that only Florence was doing anything about it. Because of his reports, Florence quickly became a heroine in Britain. A Commission of Inquiry was sent out to find out just how bad conditions were. The Commission found some dreadful things.

Florence also worked in other hospitals as well as the one at Scutari. She became seriously ill at one time, but recovered to continue her work. She wanted the soldiers to have an interest while they were recovering in hospital and brought in newspapers and journals for them to read. She also provided them with writing materials so that they could write home to their families. Many officers did not agree with this. They thought it would encourage the soldiers to be disobedient and steal the books and papers. However, this never happened.

The war ended in 1856 and Florence took a boat back to England. She was very weak after her illness and hard work and could hardly stand up by the time she returned home. Eventually she regained her strength and went back to her work. In 1860, she set up the Nightingale Training School for nurses at St Thomas's Hospital. For many years, until her death, Florence helped to run the school. Queen Victoria was so interested in her work that she invited her to Balmoral Castle to talk about the problems of health in the army. Afterwards, Queen Victoria helped Florence with her work.

Soon after this visit, however, Florence had become so weak that she became an invalid and had to continue her work from her bed. Florence continued her work to improve conditions in the army and in hospitals until her death in 1910. The whole world knew about her funeral, which was held in the small village churchyard near her parents' home. However, a grand service was also held at St Paul's Cathedral in London, where crowds came to pay their respects. Florence is still remembered because her work changed the way of life for many people, particularly soldiers. Florence also changed the idea of nursing and the lives of nurses, who came to be seen as members of an important profession. Hospitals were no longer diseased and dirty places where people merely went to die. Many pictures and statues of Florence have been made to make sure she and her work continue to be remembered.

A foot soldier's journal

14th July 1854 At last we saw land ahead and straight away orders were issued to land. We also received orders to leave behind our knapsacks, although we were allowed to take a blanket. The tents were also to be left on board the ships.

15th July 1854 We landed and began to march. There was no sign of the enemy. We stopped for the night with the rain coming down smartly on us. My two companions and myself made a good shelter from some dry grass we had quickly gathered up. I put my blanket over the top for a roof, and we did pretty well under this.

16th July 1854 There were many men soaked to the skin this morning. Some had slept in deep mud made by many feet marching in the wet weather. There were a lot of long faces because of this and also because many men had no food to eat.

I went for a bathe and on the way back was passed by some Turkish men on their way back from work. After they had passed by, an old man who was with them suddenly became ill. He fell on the ground in great pain, vomiting very much. His friends did all they could to help, but in only a few minutes the old man died. I had never seen anything like this before and wondered what it could be.

17th July 1854 I got up early and went to bathe and saw the body of the old man still there, but lying on a cart. When I got back to camp, I learned that cholera had suddenly attacked the Division. Several men were already in hospital with no hope of recovery.

Rewritten by kind permission of the Green Howards' Regimental Museum, Richmond, N Yorks. (www.greenhowards.org.uk)

■ SCHOLASTIC
PHOTOCOPIABLE

The Charge of the Light Brigade

Half a league, half a league,
Half a league onward,
All in the valley of Death
   Rode the six hundred.
"Forward, the Light Brigade!
Charge for the guns!" he said;
Into the valley of Death
   Rode the six hundred.

"Forward, the Light Brigade!"
Was there a man dismay'd?
Not tho' the soldier knew
   Some one had blunder'd:
Theirs not to make reply,
Theirs not to reason why,
Theirs but to do and die:
Into the valley of Death
   Rode the six hundred.

Cannon to right of them,
Cannon to left of them,
Cannon in front of them
   Volley'd and thunder'd;
Storm'd at with shot and shell,
Boldly they rode and well,
Into the jaws of Death,
Into the mouth of Hell
   Rode the six hundred.

Alfred, Lord Tennyson

THE GREAT FIRE OF LONDON

Content, skills and concepts

This chapter on the Great Fire of London relates to unit 5 in the QCA Scheme of Work for history at Key Stage 1, 'How do we know about the Great Fire of London?', and can be used in the planning and resourcing of the unit. Together with the Great Fire of London Resource Gallery on the CD, it introduces a range of visual and written sources that focus on this significant event from a time beyond living memory, and the famous characters associated with it.

Through previous work in history, children will already have gained experience in sequencing, the use of time-related vocabulary and using pictures and written sources. Recounting parts of stories about the past, and comparing past and present are other activities that will have introduced relevant skills and concepts needed in order to progress this unit. Suggestions for the further development of these skills form part of this chapter.

Resources on the CD-ROM

A map and pictures of London now, before and at the time of the Great Fire, an illustration of a street scene, and portraits of significant people at the time are provided on the CD-ROM. Teacher's notes containing background information about these resources are included in this chapter, along with ideas for activities.

Photocopiable pages

Photocopiable resources are provided within the book and in PDF format on the CD, from which they can be printed. They include:
▶ word cards which highlight the essential vocabulary of this topic
▶ a timeline
▶ the story of the Great Fire
▶ an extract from Samuel Pepys' diary.

The story of the fire and Pepys' account are designed to interest the children in the illustrations from the CD. They aim to enable children to make comparisons between the way fires were dealt with in the past and in the present day. The teacher's notes that accompany the photocopiable pages include suggestions for developing discussion about them and for ways of using them for whole class, group or individual activities.

History skills

Skills such as observing, describing, using time-related vocabulary, sequencing, using a timeline, comparing, inferring, speaking, reading and writing are involved in the activities provided. For example, the diary extract introduces the children to first-hand evidence and eyewitness accounts and there are opportunities to use descriptive vocabulary to describe the scenes of London burning in the pictures.

Historical understanding

In the course of the suggested tasks, a further aim is for children to begin to develop more detailed knowledge of the past and to sequence events independently through their understanding of the context and content of the factual information they use. They will begin to give reasons for the rapid spread of the fire, use sources to find further information about it and be able to recount the story. They will begin to understand that things are different in some ways from things in the past, but in other ways the same. Some more formal terminology related to chronology, such as *Stuart times*, is introduced in this chapter.

NOTES ON THE CD-ROM RESOURCES

The Great Fire

This contemporary picture of London in flames was made during the first day of the Great Fire. The picture is a similar view of London to that seen in 'St Paul's before the Great Fire' (also provided on the CD). The picture has been made using a block-printing process. It is quite a stylised image because of the need for clear lines which would print well from a woodcut. Nevertheless, this simplicity of line and stylised design of the flames gives us a good impression of the huge scale of the fire.

The fire started early on 2nd September in a baker's oven in Pudding Lane. Warm winds meant the fire spread quickly and it burned for four days. It destroyed about 13 200 houses, possibly making 100 000 people homeless. 87 out of the 109 churches in London were destroyed as well as St Paul's Cathedral.

Discussing the picture

▶ Ask the children to talk about this picture, explaining what is happening in their own words. If neccesary, point out the people in the boats.

▶ Help the children to read the text written in the corner of the picture – *London in Flames Sept 2, 1666*. Tell them why this date is significant and outline the key events of the Great Fire of London.

▶ Encourage them to think about the way the picture looks. Ask if it looks like an ordinary sketch. Discuss how at this time, many pictures were made using a simple printing method, to produce lots of copies for ordinary people to see. Explain the process of printing using a woodcut. (An image is cut in relief onto a block of wood. Only the raised areas contact the ink and make the image.)

▶ Explain that pictures like this are historical 'sources'. These visual sources are very valuable because they can show us what an event looked like to someone who may have been there at the time.

▶ Point out that London was quite small then compared to its size now. This picture shows that a very large part of London was in flames. Why do the children think the fire spread so rapidly?

▶ How do the children think the fire was eventually put out? (Controlled explosions of buildings made large breaks in the fire; the wind finally dropped and the fire died out.)

Activities

▶ Read the account of the Great Fire of London on photocopiable pages 41–2 to the children, alongside this picture.

▶ Provide block printing materials for the children to create their own fire scene in bold lines and shapes. Show them how to build up the card block, by gluing cut-paper shapes onto a piece of card, then covering the card in water-based ink and making prints.

▶ Working with a group or the whole class, compose some sentences describing the scene in the picture as if you are an eyewitness. This could be done in a modern journalistic style.

▶ Look at the pictures of '17th-century London' and 'A Stuart street scene', provided on the CD. Label the pictures to help explain the rapid spread of the fire – houses built closely together, rubbish in the streets, houses built of wood, narrow streets.

17th-century London

This is Robert Martin's lithograph of Hollar's map of London. It was made in the 17th century before the Great Fire. It does not resemble a modern map in many ways, and appears to us much more like an aerial illustration of the area. Many early maps were made in this way, with the buildings drawn on and decorative details added, such as clouds and angelic figures in the sky. Looking closely, we can make out the typical beamed structure of Tudor houses and the tall sailing ships of the period. It is a very useful illustration in the way it clearly shows how densely packed together the buildings were at the time. Not only were the houses close to each other, the map shows how little space there was between whole rows of houses, from one side of the street to the other. This was a significant feature in the rapid spread of the fire from street to street.

Discussing the map

▶ Ask the children what kind of illustration they think this is. Point out that it is, in fact, an early map of London, from the 1600s.

▶ Ask the children what they notice about the map that is very unusual. Discuss, for example, the cherubs and people in the top right-hand corner, who look rather like Native Americans. Explain that America had only fairly recently been discovered, and was a feature of great interest at the time.

▶ Get the children to identify things that they recognise, such as the Tower of London, the sailing ships, the Tudor houses and so on.

▶ Discuss any features the children notice. Particularly comment on how close together the buildings are. Discuss the implications of this in a fire; what could have happened to the flames?

Activities

▶ Compare this map with a modern map. (For example, the earlier one has pictures compared with simple lines and symbols on the modern one.)

▶ Encourage the children to observe the map closely, particularly the buildings and streets. Ask where they think the streets are in the drawing. Provide the children with drawing materials and ask them to make a 'map' in this way of their own street, for homework.

▶ Look closely at the way the houses are made. Discuss how the building materials used at that time were particularly susceptible to fire – wooden beams and walls of wattle and daub. Explain how wattle and daub is made from thin branches woven together, the spaces filled with a mixture of mud and straw – all materials likely to burn very easily in dry weather. Suggest the children bring in some twigs and provide some soft clay for them to experiment with making their own 'wattle and daub'.

▶ Ask which buildings the children think would have been less likely to burn, for example those made of stone. Give the children a simple writing frame and ask them to list the features which made some buildings dangerous in a fire, compared with those which were safer. (Wattle and daub burn easily, those made from stone burn less easily; buildings packed closely together burn rapidly; rooms containing fat and oil burn easily.)

St Paul's before the Great Fire

This illustration shows London as it was before the Great Fire. The old St Paul's Cathedral is the centrepiece of the picture, standing high above all the surrounding buildings. This 'old' St Paul's was built in the Gothic style, with tall windows, pinnacles and buttresses. Unlike the later version designed by Sir Christopher Wren, it is in the shape of a crucifix, with a long central section and two side chapels. The square tower rises above all the other church steeples and towers in London. The Thames is shown, with its Latin name, to be quite a busy thoroughfare, with boats of all sizes. Some landmarks are named on the picture, notably 'The Globe' theatre.

Discussing the illustration

▶ Show the children the illustration and discuss the period in the past that it shows. Point out how it shows London before the Great Fire, in the time known as the Stuart period. Explain that this is because the period is named after the kings and queens, whose family name was Stuart.

▶ Find out if the children think the picture was made in modern times or if they think it is an old picture. Tell them it was made at the time.

▶ Ask the children if they can see what special places the illustration shows. For example, St Paul's, the River Thames, the Globe theatre and so on.

▶ Ask volunteers to try to read the names of the places shown. Give help if necessary.

▶ Discuss the details of what can be seen, such as the river, the churches, St Paul's, ships and wharves. There is even a windmill on the left of the picture.

▶ What do the children notice about all the houses? (For example, crowded and close together.)

▶ It is difficult to tell from the picture, but explain or remind the children that, at this time, houses were usually made of wood, except the houses of the very rich.

Activities

See 'Modern London', below, for activities comparing the two pictures.

Modern London

This photograph of modern London shows how there are similarities and differences between London in the past and London of today. The buildings still seem densely packed, although we know that they are now a regulated distance apart. The River Thames is still a major feature of the city, along with its bridges. The buildings and bridge that can be seen here differ in many ways, however, from the early buildings in London before the fire. The buildings that were put up following the fire were largely made of stone. In addition to these, however, the modern constructions are made of steel and concrete. The bridge is constructed with an iron frame, painted in red and white, with stone footings. While the river is still busy as in the earlier picture, the design of the ships and boats has changed dramatically, due to the loss of sail in favour of oil-powered engines.

Discussing the photograph

▶ Ask the children if anyone can recognise this place. Where do they think this is?

▶ See if they can recognise any of the famous landmarks, such as St Paul's Cathedral and Blackfriars Bridge. What do they think the tall rectangular buildings probably are?

▶ Ask what else the children can see in the picture, for example cranes putting up even more buildings.

▶ Point out the different ships in the photograph and discuss with the children how some of them are transporting goods whilst others are for tourists and commuters.

▶ Discuss what the buildings might be made of. Ask the children if they think they look wooden.

▶ Ask how big they think the buildings are. Get them to look at the size of the trees in comparison, or to count the numbers of windows to find roughly how many floors there are in the tall buildings.

▶ See if they can find any old buildings amongst the new ones (for example on the left of the picture). Note how small they are, even St Paul's, in comparison.

Activities

▶ Help the children to place both this picture of modern London and 'St Paul's before the Great Fire' in a suitable place on a class timeline, one in the Stuart period and one in the present day.

▶ Provide the children with printouts of each picture, enough for them to work in pairs. Ask them to place the two pictures next to each other so that they can easily compare the two. What has changed since Stuart times, for example the shape of St Paul's; the type of boats on the river; the style and size of other buildings? Discuss why St Paul's is different, and why many of the old buildings have gone. Remind the children that much was burned down during the fire. A new design was used when rebuilding St Paul's, based on that of St Peter's in Rome. Look at the skyline in each picture, and note which buildings are now the tallest and appear the most important.

▶ Ask the children why the two pictures look so different, since they are both of roughly the same part of London. How were they made? (For example, one is a drawing while the other is a photograph.)

▶ Provide materials for the children to draw and paint their own pictures of St Paul's Cathedral.

▶ During shared writing, make a list of the reasons the children feel contributed towards the spread of the fire in London in Stuart times.

Portrait of Samuel Pepys

Samuel Pepys was a civil servant working to improve the navy during the Stuart period. Pepys wrote about many important events of the time including the Great Fire of London and the Plague before that. His record of events is very detailed and provides us with a major source of information about all kinds of things at this time. He also attended the court of Charles II and was a great gossip. He knew a great deal about the court and about life in London at that time – the theatres, coffee houses and gambling dens. Much of the information he learned was written in his diary, which he kept for nine years. It was written in secret and in code. The diaries were then lost and not discovered again until 1825. Luckily for posterity, Pepys was an eyewitness to the whole of the Great Fire, since he remained in London throughout, not wanting to abandon his house and belongings.

Discussing the portrait

▶ Tell the children that this is a portrait of Samuel Pepys, a famous person who lived at the time of the Great Fire of London, and who wrote about it in his diary. Explain that he was an *eyewitness* to the fire.

▶ Ask how we know that this is a painted portrait and not a photograph.

▶ Talk about the details of his appearance. What is he wearing?

▶ Look especially at his hairstyle. Explain that this was the fashion at the time.

▶ Point out what Samuel Pepys is holding. Can the children see what is on the paper? (Music.) Ask what this shows about Samuel Pepys. (He was educated and wealthy.)

Activities

▶ Ask the children if they think Samuel Pepys looks like a rich person or a poor person. Encourage them to give reasons for their decision. For example, his clothes, his neatness, the fact that he had a portrait made. Point out again that he is also educated enough to be able to read music.

▶ What sort of person do the children think Samuel Pepys was from looking at the portrait? (For example, very confident.) What is the evidence for this?

▶ Use the portrait to illustrate the account of the fire and Pepys' diary on photocopiable pages 41–2 and 43 when reading them to the children.

▶ Provide the children with sketching materials to make their own portraits. Working in pairs, ask them to draw portraits of each other. Alternatively, they could draw portraits of Samuel Pepys.

▶ Tell the children about Pepys' life in London, and about how he knew the King. Encourage them to write some sentences about Samuel Pepys to accompany their portraits of him.

▶ Ask the children to research into the life of Samuel Pepys, using both the Internet and information books.

Portrait of Charles II

Born in 1630, Charles was the second son of Charles I. After his father was beheaded on 30 January 1649 following the English Civil War, Charles escaped to France but later returned and was crowned King of the Scots. Known as Bonnie Prince Charlie, he then spent some years in hiding from Oliver Cromwell, the Puritan Lord Protector and ruler of Parliament, who had put a price on his head of £1000. Cromwell died on 3 September 1658 and the country slid into chaos. In 1660, a newly elected Parliament invited Charles to return as king. This portrait epitomises the image Charles wanted to become public. He dreamt of becoming an all-powerful ruler with his own army, acting like a god on Earth. He went to every possible length to make himself appear rich, strong and invincible, as his dress and general manner in this portrait clearly show.

Discussing the portrait

▶ What sort of picture do the children think this is? Is it a photograph? Discuss the reasons for their decision. Do they think it is a modern portrait? Why?

▶ Ask the children if they can guess what kind of person is in this picture. Do they think he is an ordinary person or someone famous and important and why is this? At this point tell them who he was.

▶ How is the King made to look important? (For example, the richness of his clothes and regalia, his attitude and manner.) Discuss the details of his costume.

▶ Discuss why Charles had this picture made, for example as a record, rather like a modern photograph album.

▶ Ask the children if they think the King looks happy, serious, stern, and so on. Discuss which words best describe his expression.

▶ Explain to the children that Charles II was a Stuart to reinforce their understanding of the term *Stuart times*.

Activities

▶ Help the children to find the correct place for Charles II on a general class timeline.

▶ Collect as many books and sources of information as possible about King Charles II, the Stuarts and the Fire of London. Encourage the children to find more portraits of Charles II and to compare them.

▶ Use the portrait to illustrate the story of the fire and the eyewitness accounts on photocopiable pages 41–3.

▶ Discuss how Charles must have felt when he saw London on fire. Help the children to compose some sentences about Charles' reactions.

▶ Provide rich materials, jewels, toy swords, and so on for the children to take on the role of Charles II. Encourage them to make up short scenes about how Charles may have acted during the Great Fire.

Portrait of Sir Christopher Wren

Christopher Wren was born in 1632 into a well-educated family and is best known today as the architect of St Paul's Cathedral. It didn't take long after the destruction of the Great Fire of London for rebuilding to begin. Wren produced a plan for restructuring London, but no plans were adopted as people preferred to rebuild it as it was. His third design for St Paul's was finally accepted. He worked on this project for most of his remaining life. The building was very innovative for the time with its huge dome being the first to be built in Britain. The work took 35 years to complete, but Wren was still alive to see the finished building, living till the age of 90.

This portrait shows him to have been slight in build, serious and thoughtful. Although wearing the rather flowing clothes fashionable at that time, Wren can be seen here to have chosen subdued, rather plain attire, in keeping with his hard-working attitude.

Discussing the portrait

▶ Tell the children that this is a picture of Sir Christopher Wren. Explain that this was the man who designed and helped to build the present-day St Paul's Cathedral. Tell them that it took 35 years.

▶ Establish why a new cathedral was needed.

▶ Ask the children why they think Wren had this portrait made. How many reasons can they think of? Ask why they think he is seated in front of this view.

▶ Encourage the children to look closely at the portrait, and then to think about how Wren appears. Ask what we can say about him from the way he is dressed.

▶ Look carefully with the children at Wren's expression. Challenge them to think of words to describe his expression, such as *serious*, *thoughtful*, and so on.

▶ From the clues in the portrait, ask them to describe the kind of person they think Wren was. Tell the children a little about his life and his interests.

▶ Explain that he is a very famous person in British history because of his innovative designs and the mathematical principles he developed for building.

Activities

▶ Place a picture or label to show Wren's life on a general class timeline.

▶ Use the portrait to illustrate discussion about what happened after the fire, when reading the account of the fire on photocopiable pages 41–2.

▶ Collect as much information as possible about Wren and the cathedral. Help the children to look up more about his life. Make a simple class book about Sir Christopher Wren. Introduce the children to the word *biography*.

▶ Look at the pictures of 'Modern London' and 'St Paul's before the Great Fire' (provided on the CD). Ask the children to identify St Paul's on each picture and to comment on the differences between the two buildings.

A Stuart street scene

Town streets during the 17th century were generally very busy places. This is a modern artist's impression of how a typical street might have looked at the time. The streets were often quite dirty, with litter on the ground and people throwing their rubbish and dirty water out of the windows of their houses. So many people were soaked in this way as they walked down the streets that it became the custom to shout *gardy loo*, derived from the French, *guardez l'eau*, meaning 'look out for the water'. Street sellers would include country people selling fruit, vegetables, chickens and game, and craftsmen selling things they had made, like pots or brushes. French traders would often cross to England to sell their garlic and onions.

Discussing the picture

▶ Ask the children to explain in their own words what they think this picture is about.
▶ Discuss in detail what they can see, such as the onion seller, the flower seller and the ducks hanging up.
▶ Ask what they think the people are throwing out of their windows. Explain about the lack of bins and drains for dirty water, and how the water was thrown into the street to run down a channel in the middle.
▶ Look at the street itself. Ask what the children think it is made from. Explain that it is a cobbled street. Ask if anyone has ever seen one like this.
▶ Discuss what other clues tell us this is a picture showing life in Stuart times. (For example, the clothes.)
▶ Link to the Great Fire by prompting the children to look at how crowded and busy the street is. Ask them to look at the buildings. *What are the buildings made from? Look at how closely they are built.*

Activities

▶ Set up a structured play area with stalls selling papier mâché fruit, paper flowers and so on. Allow time for the children to play at re-enacting the street scene they have discussed. Provide long dresses and large hats, scarves and aprons for the children to dress up and play in role.
▶ Organise a freeze-frame of the street scene with the children in role. Take a photograph of the 'image' the children create.
▶ Talk about how this picture is different from modern streets in towns. How is it the same? Ask the children to write down at least three differences and similarities.
▶ Work with the children on a list of adjectives to describe how it would be like in this street. Ask: *What would it smell like? Would it be noisy? How might you feel?* Then use the adjectives to compose some sentences to describe the street scene and display them with the picture.

NOTES ON THE PHOTOCOPIABLE PAGES

Word cards   PAGES 35–9

A number of specific types of vocabulary have been introduced on the word cards:
▶ words related to the passing of time and chronology, such as *a very long time ago, century*
▶ words associated with buildings and fires, such as *timber, thatch, flames, burned*
▶ words to describe reasons and results, such as *because, effect*
▶ words associated with sources of information, such as *eyewitness, account, woodcut*.
Encourage the children to think of appropriate words to add to those provided, to build up a word bank with which to discuss the theme of the Great Fire of London. They could also use the cards in displays, in matching activities and to help them in writing captions for pictures. Once you have made copies of the word cards, cut them out and laminate them. Use them as often as possible when talking about the Great Fire of London or for word games.

Activities

▶ Make displays of firefighters at different times in the past and in the present and use the word cards to label them, for example *modern*.
▶ Begin to encourage the children, during whole class lessons, to think of sentences using the words they have learned to read.
▶ Ask the children to use the reasons and results word cards to describe how the fire started and why it spread so quickly.
▶ The buildings word cards could be used to compare old and modern pictures of London, to compare the two St Paul's, and to explain why the fire spread so quickly.
▶ Give out sets of the fire word cards to children to use to help them write sentences describing the fire or describing what Pepys saw.
▶ The information sources word cards would be useful when talking about 'The Great Fire' woodcut (provided on the CD) and Pepys' diary extract (see photocopiable page 43).

Timeline of the Great Fire of London

PAGE 40

This timeline can be used to introduce children to the notion of chronology over a short span of time, in this case, just a few days. It is a simple timeline for children to understand and they are likely to be able to make up their own sequence or timeline of the Great Fire with more detail.

The kind of timeline shown here can also be useful at the end of the topic, for checking children's success in grasping ideas of sequence, chronology and, for those at that stage, understanding of the use of dates. This could also be carried out by asking them to create their own version of the timeline.

Discussing the timeline

▶ At the beginning of the topic, ask the children what they think this timeline shows.

▶ Clarify what the dates on the timeline mean. Look at the 'reading direction' of the timeline. Explain that this represents the passing of time.

▶ Talk about the events during the fire (use the account of the fire on photocopiable pages 41–2) and add more labels as appropriate.

▶ Use the pictures provided on the CD to illustrate the discussion about the timeline.

Activities

▶ Make a class timeline using the timeline provided on photocopiable page 40 as an example. Ask children to put on any other pictures of the Great Fire they find. Also give them pictures from the CD to put in the appropriate places on the timeline.

▶ Give the children a blank timeline with either relevant dates or words and ask them to draw pictures of the fire, or paste on pictures of it.

▶ Show the children how to convert a timeline into a time chart. Divide a chart into two columns – one for the dates, the other for what happened on those dates – for the children to create a time chart by transferring information to it from the timeline and other sources.

Account of the Great Fire of London

PAGES 41–2

This account provides some details of what happened during each day when the fire was at its worst. It makes use of Pepys' diary to mention the activities of other people involved. These included King Charles II, the mayor (Sir Thomas Bludworth) and the Duke of York (the King's brother whom he put in charge of the city). The King seems to have tried his best to get some preventative measures organised, but the Mayor seems to have been unable or unwilling to carry out his orders. He came out of it a very unpopular Lord Mayor. The Duke of York appears to have been the only person able to act decisively, using his soldiers to pull down buildings and douse the flames in some successful attempts to stop the fire spreading.

Discussing the account

▶ Read through an enlarged copy of the account with the class.

▶ Ask the children what words they find difficult to understand, for example *raged, surrounding, maid, cellars*. Explain the meaning of the words.

▶ Re-read the account and see if the children can add any other details from their own knowledge of events during the fire.

▶ Compare how fires were dealt with in the past and in the present day, for example during the Great Fire of London, the authorities ordered soldiers to pull houses down to stop the fire from spreading. Today, the fire brigade would be called by ringing 999 on a telephone. (Remind the children that they must only ring this number in an emergency.)

Activities

▶ Help the children to locate the fire on a large-scale timeline of British history. Add pictures and labels. Look at the order of the dates in the account and compare these with the timeline. Note the regular pattern of describing each day in turn.

▶ Use the pictures and portraits from the CD to illustrate the reading.

▶ Children could make a large collage showing the silhouettes of the buildings and the flames superimposed over them. Suggest they use brightly coloured tissue paper for the flames and black for the sky.

▶ Encourage the children to retell the events of the Great Fire in their own words, or write a shorter version of it on their own. Start off some sentences for them.

▶ Challenge the children, working in pairs, to find further information about the fire. Set questions such as: *How many churches were burned down? How many homes were destroyed? How many people were left homeless?*

▶ Find the places mentioned in the story on a modern street map of London, for example Pudding Lane, the Tower of London.

Extract from Pepys' diary

PAGE 43

This short extract is quite difficult for young children to understand. They will need support in making sense of some of the vocabulary and some of the expressions used in it. However, it is a useful detail for them to see, because it describes clearly the terrible panic that people must have experienced. It also shows how desperate the poor people were at the prospect of losing their homes, since they would not be able to get another one. The poor had very little support in those days. Pepys is a master at pointing out the really heart-rending details, such as the pigeons being afraid to leave, rather like the poor, and burning their wings.

Discussing the extract

▶ Read the extract to the children twice so that they can become used to the archaic style of writing. Ask when they think this was written. A very long time ago? Recently?

▶ Ask the children what they think this piece of writing is about. Can they guess what type of text it is taken from and who wrote it?

▶ Ask if they know why Pepys wrote this down. What were his reasons? (He realised this was an important event and he wanted to record it for the future.)

▶ Look at the difficult words, such as *lighters, clambering, perceive, loath, hovered*. Explain the meaning of these words and re-read the sentences and then the whole extract.

▶ Discuss how this is an *eyewitness account* and what these words mean. Talk about how Pepys was there and saw the fire with his own eyes.

Activities

▶ Encourage the children to retell the events described by Pepys in their own words.

▶ Provide painting and drawing materials for the children to make their own imaginary pictures of the scene Pepys describes.

▶ Give different roles to each child and then organise the class into a freeze-frame, some in the act of rushing away with their things, while others are afraid and stay behind. Allow time for the children to work at a small scene, re-enacting the events described in the extract.

▶ Select other short extracts from Pepys' diary to read to and with the class to extend their understanding of an archaic style of writing and the unusual vocabulary he used. What other events does he talk about in his diary? (For example, the return to London of the bubonic plague in 1665.)

▶ Encourage the children to find out more about Samuel Pepys' life. Provide them with information books and access to the Internet. Look at the 'Portrait of Samuel Pepys' provided on the CD.

▶ Ask the children to write their own diary entry, imagining they were living in London at the time the fire broke out. Model the first couple of sentences to start them off, for example: *I got up this morning to a terrible sight. From my bedroom window I could see...* Provide them with copies of the time, buildings and fire word cards on photocopiable pages 35–7 to assist them, if necessary.

Find the right ending

PAGE 44

These 'heads and tails' are based closely on the kind of material which the children will be very familiar with by the end of the topic. It is therefore suggested that they complete this writing frame once they have acquired this knowledge. The activity can be surprisingly difficult for some children, so they will need support until they understand how to match the sentence beginnings and endings.

Time word cards

a very long time ago
began
when
century
modern
first
next
finally

Buildings word cards

timber
frame
plaster
thatch
church
abbey
cathedral
rebuilt

Fire word cards

flames
roaring
sparks
heat
smoke
belching
burned
destroyed

Reasons and results word cards

because

reason

result

effect

why

◣SCHOLASTIC
PHOTOCOPIABLE

Information sources word cards

eyewitness

diary

firsthand

woodcut

account

source

evidence

Great Fire of London timeline

Ancient Art and Architecture Collection Ltd

LONDON in Flames Sept. 2, 1666

the fire breaks out

2nd September 1666

the fire spreads

3rd and 4th September 1666

the fire dies out

5th September 1666

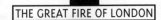

Account of the Great Fire of London

On the 2nd of September, 1666, the worst fire ever to have raged in London burned down a large part of the city. It is known as 'the Great Fire of London'. It is said to have started at a baker's shop in Pudding Lane in the heart of London. The oven caught fire and the flames were fanned by a strong wind. The fire then spread rapidly through the building and into the surrounding shops and houses. The weather had been very dry for a long time and this made everything burn faster. Also, the houses were built very close together. This meant that the fire could easily leap from one house to the next, especially where they almost touched each other.

Samuel Pepys was in London at the time of the fire and was woken up by his maid, Jane, who told him about it. During the day he went out to the Tower of London, where he climbed up high to see as far as he could. He saw a huge fire burning down everything in its path. He heard that the fire had burned down a church and most of Fish Street even on the first day. Pepys then went to see the King, who said that the only way to stop the fire was to pull down the houses in its path. The King sent Pepys with orders for the Lord Mayor to do this.

When Pepys found him, the Mayor was in a terrible state. He had been up all night trying to stop the fire and now people were not doing what he asked. He decided he needed a rest and went home, leaving all the people to look after themselves.

As Pepys walked home later he saw people running about trying to save their things from the fire. There was no one working to put it out. The fire was getting stronger and fiercer all the time. Cellars full of oil and wines were burning even more fiercely than the rest and adding to the strength of the spreading flames.

Account of the Great Fire of London (cont)

Pepys and many others were not able to sleep that night. When he went out to look, he found his face was burned with showers of fire-drops, and the air was full of smoke. He heard a terrible noise from the flames and cracking sounds as the houses burned and fell down.

The next day, people were still busy trying to move their things away from the fire. Pepys also moved his best things to a friend's house further away from the fire. The streets and the river were full of people rushing away with as much as they could carry. By the 4th of September, the fire was getting very close to Pepys' house. People could no longer find anywhere to put their things for safety. Some decided to bury their wine, papers and even cheese in their gardens, hoping that this would save them from burning.

By the 5th of September, people were feeling very weary. Pepys says in his diary how he could hardly stand, he was so tired. He had eaten very little except cold scraps for some time. After all this time, the fire had destroyed a great part of London, including many famous old buildings. Among these was St Paul's Cathedral. This had been one of the largest buildings in London and now it was turned to ashes. People were beginning to say that maybe some kind of enemy had started the fires, which kept leaping up in different parts of the city. Some said it was the French and others blamed the Catholics.

The next day still saw small fires starting in different places, but the Duke of York brought his soldiers and they worked to put them out before they could spread. By the 7th of September, the fire was mostly out. Samuel Pepys describes how he saw all the town burned, and a miserable sight of St Paul's with all the roofs fallen in. Small fires continued to burn for a long time, but the worst of the fire was over.

■ SCHOLASTIC
PHOTOCOPIABLE

Extract from Pepys' diary

2nd September, 1666

So down I went, with my heart full of trouble, to the Lieutenant of the Tower, who tells me that it began this morning in the King's baker's house in Pudding Lane, and that it hath burned St Magnus's Church and most part of Fish Street already. So I rode down to the waterside... and there saw a lamentable fire... Everybody endeavouring to remove their goods, and flinging into the river, or bringing them into lighters that lay off; poor people staying in their houses as long as till the very fire touched them, and then running into boats, or clambering from one pair of stairs by the water-side to another. And among other things, the poor pigeons, I perceive, were loath to leave their houses, but hovered about the windows and balconies, till they burned their wings, and fell down.

see www.pepys.info/fire.htm

Find the right ending

▷ Here are some beginnings and endings of sentences. See if you can match them up and then write them out correctly.

Beginnings

The Great Fire of London spread quickly because

The people tried to escape from the fire

They went to the churches because

Samuel Pepys could see the fire

Pepys watched the fire and wrote about it

Endings

they were built of stone and did not burn so easily.

in his diary.

from his house.

the houses were made of wood and burned easily.

in the river or in the churches.

📖 SCHOLASTIC
PHOTOCOPIABLE

REMEMBRANCE DAY

Content, skills and concepts
This chapter relates to unit 17 in the QCA Scheme of Work for history for Year 2, 'What are we remembering on Remembrance Day?'. The chapter assists with planning and resourcing the unit and, together with the Remembrance Day Resource Gallery on the CD, it introduces a range of visual and written sources that can be used in teaching about this significant anniversary. It allows for comparison of Remembrance Day in the past with present-day ceremonies and why this event takes place every year. In the course of this explanation, some detail about the First World War is introduced. Some of the photographs showing images from the war will need to be handled sensitively.

Resources on the CD-ROM
Photographs of poppies and the poppy makers, of battlefields and of soldiers in the First World War are provided on the CD-ROM as well as photographs of war memorials and cemeteries. Teacher's notes containing background information about these resources are included in this chapter. Also on the CD-ROM is a video clip of a Remembrance Day service held in 1945. This will involve the children with looking at real-life experiences from the past in a meaningful format.

Before looking at the resources, send out a letter to families and carers asking for any wartime memorabilia that they might be willing to loan for a short time. These items can then be used to illustrate the photographs and to give the children firsthand experience of some of the things from the war.

Photocopiable pages
Photocopiable resources are provided within the book and in PDF format on the CD from which they can be printed. They include:
▶ word cards highlighting the essential vocabulary of this topic
▶ a timeline of WWI
▶ the poem 'In Flanders Fields' by John McCrae
▶ letters from soldiers at the time of the First World War.
Teacher's notes are provided in this chapter to accompany all the photocopiable pages.

The account of World War I and the soldiers' letters about conditions at the time are designed to interest the children in the resources on the CD, and to introduce them to notions of the past. They also aim to show the children why we have Remembrance Day and who we are remembering. It is important to stress that it is not just WWI we are remembering, but all wars that have occured since then in which Britain has played a part.

History skills
Skills such as observing, describing, using time-related vocabulary, sequencing, comparing, using a timeline, inferring, listening, speaking, reading and writing are involved in the activities provided. For example, there is an opportunity to develop independent skills in observing, describing and comparing when watching the video of a 1945 Remembrance Day service.

Historical understanding
In the course of the suggested tasks, a further aim is for children to begin to develop a more detailed knowledge of the past and their ability to sequence events independently, through their understanding of the context and content of the factual information they use. Some of the more precise terminology related to chronology is introduced in this chapter, for example dates like *1914* and *1918*.

NOTES ON THE CD-ROM RESOURCES

Remembrance Day poppy

Poppies like the one in this photograph are sold on Remembrance Day each year for people to wear in memory of those who lost their lives in the two great wars and all the other terrible wars of the last century. The money raised goes to help look after the wounded soldiers from the first and second world wars, and from any recent war. The tradition of associating the poppy with war began following the publication of a war poem by John McCrae during the First World War. Poppies grew profusely in the fields in Belgium where much of the heavy fighting took place in the first war, and where many soldiers lost their lives. It was the scenes of poppies growing amongst the graves of dead soldiers in these fields that inspired McCrae, a Canadian soldier, to include them in his poem, 'In Flanders Fields' (see photocopiable page 62). Ever since, the poppy has been adopted as the symbol for commemorating the war dead, in this country and many others.

Discussing the photograph

▶ Ask the children if they have seen a poppy like this before. Where have they seen it? When?

▶ Ask if they think it looks like a real poppy. Compare it with those in the photograph of the poppy field on the CD.

▶ Discuss how the poppy is made. (It is made by hand in a small factory often by disabled soldiers from past wars. They make the poppy flowers from stiff paper and then push through the green plastic stem to hold everything together.)

▶ Find out if any of the children know why people sell and wear these poppies each year. Explain that this happens every year in November. If they do not know, explain that it is to commemorate the soldiers who died fighting in the great wars. Talk about how they would have wanted us to remember them and how they died to save their country from invasion.

▶ Explain how soldiers from many parts of the world fought for the Allies in both wars and how those countries all use poppies as a way of remembering them.

Activities

▶ Help the children to find and label the right place for the First World War on a general class timeline of British history.

▶ Look at a map of Europe and find Belgium and France, where most of the fighting took place.

▶ Read the poem, 'In Flanders Fields', on photocopiable page 62 to the class. Talk about how the poppy was made into a famous symbol when this poem became known.

▶ During a shared writing session, compose some simple rhyming lines about the poppy.

▶ Provide some thin card for the children to make their own poppies.

Poppy field

This photograph shows a French poppy field like those in McCrae's poem (see photocopiable page 62). In France and Belgium at this time, the poppies grew everywhere in the fields and struck a poignant chord when the men saw them growing amongst the graves of their dead comrades. It was a surprise to see these red flowers growing so thickly just where their friends had died, and people were not sure why this happened. One theory is that possibly, the digging of the earth in burying the dead turned over the soil, enabling the poppies to seed very easily, resulting in a mass of them coming into bloom.

Discussing the photograph

▶ Ask the children what they can see in the photograph. What do they think is growing in the field? Can they identify the poppies?

▶ Ask the children if they think these are real poppies. How do they know?

▶ Explain that the real poppies growing in the fields around the battlefields during the First World War inspired a soldier called John McCrae to write his famous poem 'In Flanders Fields'. Explain how this poem led to the adoption of the poppy as a symbol of remembrance of soldiers who died during wartime.

▶ Talk about why the choice of a flower seems very appropriate as a symbol of remembrance. (For example, the poppies bloom every year – they are a symbol of life continuing despite what has happened.)
▶ Ask the children about important things that they remember. Explain that their own memories are a kind of history too.
▶ Show the children on a map of Europe the areas where fighting took place – north-west France and Belgium.

Activities
▶ See if the children can remember the date of Remembrance Day (Poppy Day) and remind them of it if they cannot remember.
▶ Read together the poem 'In Flanders Fields' on photocopiable page 62 whilst looking at the photograph.
▶ Provide a variety of drawing media, such as pastels, for the children to draw their own poppy fields.
▶ Compose with the class some simple sentences about why we remember the dead soldiers.
▶ Find other pictures of poppies and poppy fields – see also 'Poppy' and 'Remembrance Day poppy' (provided on the CD) – and make a display, along with the children's drawings and writing about Remembrance Day.

Making poppies

The poppies that people wear or that are used to make wreaths are made in the poppy factory at Richmond near London or at the Haig Poppy Factory in Edinburgh, as shown in this photograph. A hundred people work in the factory and others work at home, making more poppies. The small poppies are made from paper with plastic stems. The larger ones are made from silk, with wire stems. The money that is made from selling the poppies is collected by the British Legion, an organisation which helps care for wounded soldiers and the families of people who fought in wars. The British Legion then uses the money to help with all this care.

This photograph, taken in 1952, shows the workers making special wreaths and tributes which will be used in large memorial services all over the country. Many of the people who worked in the poppy factory at this time were soldiers who had been wounded in the war and then found it hard to work at an ordinary job when the war was over.

Discussing the photograph
▶ Ask the children to point out the poppies in the picture.
▶ Ask who they think the people are that are making them.
▶ The people here are not just making the poppies. What else do the children think they are making? Explain why larger items are being made.
▶ Ask the children if they think this picture was taken a long time ago or recently. Discuss how they know. What are the clues? For example, the dress of the men.

Activities
▶ Organise the children into small groups and ask them to look for more pictures or simple information about the making of poppies and the British Legion.
▶ Link this picture with 'A war memorial' (provided on the CD). What is the woman doing? (Laying a poppy wreath.) Watch the video 'Armistice Day, 1945' and in particular the laying of the poppy wreaths.
▶ Provide the children with materials to make their own poppy wreaths. They could use the card poppies they made in the activities for 'Remembrance Day poppy', above.

A war memorial

This photograph was taken at a Remembrance Day ceremony in 1947, two years after the Second World War ended. Remembrance Day services are held on the Sunday closest to November 11th, which is Armistice Day, the day on which fighting stopped in 1918. The service shown in this photograph took place in the village of Wimpole, Cambridgeshire and is typical of services that were, and still are, carried out around the country to honour the dead from both world wars.

Discussing the photograph

▶ Ask the children if they recognise the place where the wreaths are being laid. Is there a similar monument near to the school or where they live? Explain that after the First World War monuments like this were built in every town and village to commemorate those who were killed.

▶ What is the woman in the picture doing? What is a *wreath*?

▶ Suggest the children look closely at the wreaths in this photograph. Ask what flowers have been used to make these. Can they see the poppy wreath? Do they know why poppies are used?

▶ Talk about the special ceremony in London, at the Cenotaph. Explain what this word means. (Empty tomb.) Tell the children about the Unknown Solider.

▶ Ask if they can guess what time of year this service is taking place. (For example, winter because of the people's warm clothes.) Explain that the service is held in November, because that was when the First World War came to an end. Mention also that we remember soldiers killed in other wars too on this day, not just World War I.

Activities

▶ Find out about the memorial ceremony at the Cenotaph in London. Which important people go to this ceremony?

▶ Find out about your local Remembrance Day service. Who goes to this? What happens?

▶ Visit your local memorial. What information is recorded on it? Ask the children to sketch it on site and then draw more detailed drawings back in the classroom.

▶ Watch the video 'Armistice Day 1945' (provided on the CD) and compare what is happening with what is happening in the photograph. Do the same things occur in Remembrance services today?

War graves

These war graves are at the Tyne Cot cemetery near Ypres, Belgium. Special military graveyards were made in various parts of Europe where the soldiers could all be buried with dignity. The people who live in towns and villages nearby still keep these cemeteries immaculate. Many people still visit them, sometimes making special journeys, just to see the graves, or perhaps to visit the grave of someone they knew. Those who visit the cemeteries are often surprised and shocked at their size, the hundreds of thousands of graves and the eerie silence of these places. The sight impresses on people the terrible waste of war.

Discussing the photograph

▶ Ask the children if they can understand what this photograph shows.

▶ Why do they think there are so many gravestones?

▶ What do the children notice about the graveyard. Is it like the graveyards they see in their own towns and villages? Ask what makes it different.

▶ Ask how many graves they think may be here. Explain that many thousands of people are buried in graves like these.

▶ Mention the Tomb of the Unknown Soldier. Explain that there are many memorials built to Unknown Soldiers in many countries around the world. In these tombs, a candle burns forever on the graves. Discuss why the soldiers are 'unknown' and ask the children if they can understand why there are graves like this. Explain that many soldiers died, but were never identified. Sometimes there was no time to make special graves for each one. So now there is a tomb like this so that we can remember soldiers like these, buried on the battlefields and with no proper graves of their own.

Activities

▶ If possible, take a walk around your own local graveyard. Notice what the tombstones and graves are like. Back at school, compare these findings with the picture. Note the significant differences between the two, for example in the photograph, the gravestones are all identical and in rows.

▶ Ask the children for their reactions to the image. Provide the beginnings of sentences for the children to complete, such as, *The picture makes us feel...*

▶ Read the poem 'In Flanders Fields' on photocopiable page 62, which was written very near to the battlefields of Ypres.

Gunners

These gunners were photographed in action at the Somme during the First World War. As can be seen from the picture, the guns were heavy and very large, making them difficult to manoeuvre. The gunners had a vitally important role in battles, since they had to weaken the enemy before the foot soldiers were sent in. This was dangerous work, however, and the gunners would often come under attack themselves because they were so near to the front-line fighting and their position was known to the enemy due to the firing. It was also in the enemy's interest to 'take out' the gunners to minimise the damage caused to their own troops.

Discussing the picture

▶ Ask the children what kind of source this is. Is it a photograph, painting or drawing? How do they know?

▶ Ask if they think it is a recent picture. Again, how can they tell? Point out that it is a photograph from the First World War. Look closely at the soldiers' uniforms. Do they look like modern uniforms?

▶ Do they think that these fairly ordinary clothes seem suitable for the job the soldiers are doing. What do they think modern soldiers would wear?

▶ Discuss what the soldiers are firing at. Talk about the dangers of this particular role in the fighting.

Activities

▶ Help the children to locate 1914 and 1918 on the class timeline. Draw in a span to show that the war continued throughout these years.

▶ Ask the children to find out about the different types of soldiers who fought in the First World War. What were their particular duties?

▶ If possible, take the children to one of the military museums or collections, such as the Imperial War Museum.

▶ Talk about what it must have been like for the men working with these huge guns. Discuss the sounds. Make a display of words that children suggest to represent the sounds of war.

German trenches

This photograph was taken from the German trenches on the Western Front during the First World War. Although dreadful to live in, these trenches provided some refuge from the bombs and bullets that were coming over from the enemy side. Unlike the gunners, other troops spent most of their time at the front hidden down in these trenches. The troops in this picture seem a long way away from any action, but this was deceptive. Bullets and shells travelled a long way, and soldiers were warned to keep their heads down at all times. During lulls in the firing, however, they would peep out, like the German soldier in the foreground of this photograph. Sometimes they would wave and shout to the troops on the other side. On one famous occasion on Christmas day, both sides put down their guns, left their trenches and walked across to shake hands.

Discussing the photograph

▶ Look carefully at the photograph and get the children to point out who and what they can see.

▶ Explain to the children that this is a photograph of the trenches during the First World War and that it is taken from the German side.

▶ Ask the children if they can work out why the soldiers had to be in these trenches. Why were they made?

▶ What do the children notice about the uniform and helmet the soldiers are wearing?

▶ Ask why they think the ground looks so bare. Why is there smoke in the distance?

▶ What do the children think it must have been like? Ask how they think they would have felt.

Activities

▶ Read the account of the First World War on photocopiable page 61. Use this picture and others like it from the CD to illustrate the story. They may also be useful to illustrate the soldiers' letters on photocopiable page 63.

▶ Talk about how the conditions and experiences of the German soldiers was very much the same as for the British troops – see 'British trench' (provided on the CD), and how it was bad for all of them. Try to avoid bias and to introduce a balanced view of the war.

▶ Look up where Germany is on a map of Europe.

▶ Make a collection of words and phrases which capture the children's feelings about the pictures, for example the sounds, sights and emotions they think the soldiers might have experienced. Use these in composing some short imaginative pieces with them.

▶ Set up a role-play, where some children have the role of British soldiers and others are German and re-enact the moment when the two sides decided to put down their weapons and wish each other a happy Christmas.

▶ Make a large collage of a scene like this. Add, at a safe distance from the children's reach, some barbed wire for them to see other dangers which the soldiers faced.

Officers at the front line

This picture shows officers of the King's Liverpool Regiment at the front line in the First World War. The picture is interesting in the way it shows details of the inside of a trench. This one appears to be well boarded and includes boards on the ground to prevent the soldiers' feet getting soaked in the mud.

Discussing the photograph

▶ Tell the class that this is a picture of some officers in the trenches. Ask the children who officers were and how they were different from the other soldiers.

▶ Look carefully at the inside of the trench. Get the children to describe how they think the trench was made.

▶ Ask the children to point out details of the officers' uniforms. What is the same and what is different from modern military dress?

▶ Challenge the children to find all the different weapons that the officers have with them.

▶ Ask if the class can guess what the officers are doing. (Deciding on battle tactics.) Ask what the officers would do next. (For example, give orders to the rest of the men.)

Activities

▶ Ask the children to research the different ranks of officers that were in the army during the First World War. Explain how all these different people had their own special position of importance.

▶ Look at the soldier shown in 'British trench'. Are the officers' uniforms different from this soldiers'?

▶ Devise a short role-play based on what might be happening in this picture. What might the officers be discussing? What could be written or shown on the piece of paper? Do they look as if they are under fire?

British trench

Here we can see what conditions were like for the soldiers living in the trenches. This is a photograph of a British soldier in a flooded dugout in a front-line trench near Ploegsteert Wood in Belgium, at some point during the First World War. Soldiers had to live in these conditions for much of the war. It was difficult for them to keep dry or clean. Often the trenches were full of rats which would get into their clothes and food. Many soldiers became ill because of these conditions and because of the noise of shells exploding nearby.

Discussing the photograph

▶ Ask the children what they think has happened here. Why do they think the soldier is in this deep water?

▶ Explain how the trenches were often flooded like this. Also explain that the trenches were where the soldiers had to live, eat and sleep. Explain how they frequently slept in the mud, in wet clothes, and how there were rats in the trenches.

▶ What do the children think the bags are for that he is leaning against? Explain how sand bags are used to make a temporary wall, in an attempt to keep out some of the water.

▶ Ask how the children think the soldiers must have felt living in places like this. Explain how they were often unwell.

Activities
▶ Use this photograph to illustrate the 'Account of The First World War' on page 61 and the 'Soldiers' letters' on page 63.
▶ Organise the children to work in small groups to discuss the conditions the soldier is in here. Get them to choose one person to write a description of what life was like for him.
▶ Imagine the soldier in the photograph is writing home to his children. Make up some sentences, with the class, that he might have put in his letter.
▶ Compare this image with 'German trenches' (provided on the CD). Explain that although we can't see water in the German trenches, conditions were the same for both armies.

Field dressing station

This photograph shows dead and wounded soldiers lying at a dressing station in the Somme region during the First World War. This was where some of the worst fighting took place and where many men were killed. It was difficult for the medical services to cope with the huge number of wounded, and so many were left to lie in the fields in all weathers. You may need to handle the use of this picture sensitively since some children may find it disturbing.

Discussing the photograph
▶ Ask the children what they think has happened to the soldiers in this picture.
▶ Explain that this is called a dressing station. This is where soldiers were taken to have their wounds dressed when they were injured.
▶ Ask what the soldiers are lying on.
▶ Look closely at the picture, and note how some soldiers have blankets, but not all of them. Ask why this is. (Perhaps there were not enough blankets to go round.)
▶ How easy would it be for medical staff to treat patients in these conditions?
▶ Talk about how it was scenes like these that led John McCrae to write 'In Flanders Fields' (see photocopiable page 62). Explain that he was a doctor as well as a soldier and worked in a dressing station like this one.

Activities
▶ Set up a structured play area, with space for the 'wounded' and with doctors and nurses to tend them. Provide props such as walking sticks, bandages, and so on.
▶ Compose some verses about the dangers of war. Write the first few lines together with the class and then let the children write some of their own.
▶ Challenge the children to write their own story of the First World War.

Video: Armistice Day, 1945

This (silent) video clip shows the important people of the town of Boston, Lincolnshire laying wreaths at the war memorial and making speeches as part of an Armistice Day ceremony. This type of service might take place in any area across the country. We see the Mayor laying the first wreath, made of poppies. Then, wreaths are laid by the chief members of the civil service and representatives of each of the armed forces. The crowds and police are still and appear to be silent, in awe and respect of the seriousness of this occasion. Accompanied by lawyers in their wigs and dignitaries in their top hats, the group then processes through the town to another place where they make speeches. The Home Guard are prominent in their tin hats and pass their flag to the Mayor before he begins to speak. The whole occasion helps to instil in the viewer the momentousness of the events that were taking place at that time, made all the more poignant by the fact that the Second World War had only just ended.

Discussing the video
▶ Once the children have taken in the events shown in the video clip, ask them what they think is happening. Get them to describe what they have understood.
▶ Explain how the video is in three parts: the laying of wreaths; processing through the town; making speeches.
▶ Why do the children think the people in the video are all dressed so differently, for example the top hats, wigs, military uniforms and so on. Why do some of them wear medals?
▶ What is Armistice Day? Discuss the meaning and significance of this day.

Activities

▶ Provide costumes and props for the children to mime or re-enact the scene they have watched.

▶ As part of a shared writing session, write a paragraph about why Remembrance Day was so important to people at the time. Add another explaining why it is still important to a lot of people now.

▶ Can any of the children talk about Remembrance Day services they have been to? Did they see any people lay poppy wreaths? Who were these people?

NOTES ON THE PHOTOCOPIABLE PAGES

Word cards
PAGES 55–9

A number of specific types of vocabulary have been introduced on the word cards:

▶ words related to the passing of time and everyday words, such as *now*, *then*, *a very long time ago*, *first*, *second*, *1918*

▶ words associated with commemoration, such as *remembrance*, *anniversary*, *veteran*

▶ words associated with specific events, such as *World War I*, *World War II*, *ceasefire*, *conflict*

▶ words associated with types of evidence, such as *memorial*, *eyewitness*, *account*.

Encourage the children to think of other appropriate words to add to these, in order to build up a wordbank for the theme of Remembrance Day. They could also use the cards in displays, and to help them in writing captions for their pictures. Once you have made copies of the word cards, cut them out and laminate them, use them as often as possible when talking about Remembrance Day or for word games associated with the theme.

Activities

▶ Add further vocabulary to the set of words, using suggestions from the children, for example *fighting*, *wounded*, *battles*, *doctors*, *nurses*. The children may also want to add words associated with their feelings when looking at the pictures of war graves, trenches and poppies.

▶ Encourage the children to match the words to the pictures on the CD as often as possible. For example, provide groups of pictures and ask the children to choose word cards that describe them.

■ Begin to encourage the children, during whole class lessons, to think of and write sentences that include the key words they have learned.

▶ Make new sets of word cards related to topics such as sources of information. These might include words like *diary*, *report*, *account*.

First World War timeline
PAGE 60

The aim of this timeline is primarily to introduce young children to the idea of a sequence of events presented in chronological order and to begin to introduce, as appropriate, a small number of significant dates. This timeline could be used in conjunction with the story of the war, to give children some visual representation of the chronological sequence of key events. It could be adapted for the classroom in the form of a long string stretched across the room, to represent the distance in time covered during the war. The kind of timeline shown here can also be useful at the end of the topic, for checking children's success in grasping ideas of sequence, chronology and, for those at that stage, understanding of the use of dates.

Discussing the timeline

▶ At the beginning of the topic, ask the class what they think this timeline shows.

▶ Discuss what the numbers on the timeline mean.

▶ Look at the 'reading direction' of the timeline. Show how the numbers are bigger as you read along. Explain that this means time is passing.

▶ Add more dates to the line. Show how a timeline can be rather like a number line, but it means more than a simple line of numbers. It can include months and days. Explain how it represents the passing of years.

Activities

▶ Make a class timeline using this one as an example. Ask children to put on any other pictures of the war that they find, in the appropriate places on the timeline.

▶ Get the children to read out the dates and practise saying them correctly. Remind them of the current year and how we say this as a date. See if they can tell you some other dates from the past.

▶ Challenge very able children to work out how long ago these things happened, and how long the war lasted.

Account of the First World War   PAGE 61

This simple account aims to give an initial understanding of soldiers' experiences in the First World War. It limits the use of dates and factual information, focusing instead on the human issues involved. It explains some of the experiences of the young men who went to fight as soldiers, and their growing realisation that the war was not as they had expected it to be. It gives some explanation of why and how the poppy began to be used as a symbol of remembrance.

Discussing the account

▶ Read the text as part of a shared reading session, using the timeline to find the dates of the beginning and end of the war.

▶ Ask the children which people in their own families would have been alive at this time. (For example, the children's great great grandparents.) Ask how long ago this was.

▶ What kind of people were keen to go to war, and what did they find when they got to France?

▶ Where did the soldiers have to live when they were at war?

▶ Ask for volunteers to explain in their own words why the poppy is still used as a symbol of remembrance.

Activities

▶ Ask the children to write their own version of the account.

▶ Provide the children with materials to paint some vivid pictures of war.

▶ Talk about other commemorative days, such as November 5th which remembers Guy Fawkes' failed attempt to blow up the Houses of Parliament. Compare these with Remembrance Day. Discuss how these 'anniversaries' are celebrated every year. Make a list of the special days the children know of, including their own birthdays. These could be put onto a timeline of one year.

▶ Look at the photographs 'Gunners', 'British trench', 'Field dressing station' and 'War graves' (provided on the CD) in conjunction with this text.

In Flanders Fields   PAGE 62

John McCrae, a Canadian doctor and soldier in the First World War, wrote this poem in 1915 in a quiet moment whilst in the back of an ambulance parked near the dressing station of Ypres in the Flanders region of Belgium. He wrote it after being particularly affected by the death of a young friend who had been killed by a shell burst. McCrae was aware of all the dangers and of the suffering of the men, and no doubt feared what might happen to himself. He was eventually wounded and taken away from the battlefield. However, he died in service just before the end of the war.

The poem is a challenging read for young children so you will need to read it several times and provide considerable support in understanding some of the vocabulary and ensuring the children can follow the meaning.

Discussing the poem

▶ Discuss the title of the poem with the children. Look at a map to find Ypres, where McCrae wrote the poem.

▶ Read the poem to and with the children.

▶ Encourage the children to notice and pick out the rhyming words.

▶ Point out how the sentences do not end at the end of each line. For example, look at the first two and a half lines to see how they need to be read together to make sense.

▶ Get the children to think about who is the narrator. How can he be dead? Talk about what point of view the poem is written from.

▶ Consider why McCrae has chosen flowers and birds (larks) to write about. (For example, they are alive, while the men are dead.)

▶ Remind the children of the important date of Remembrance Day, November 11th, which is the same each year. Explain how it is an anniversary of the ending of the war.

Activities

▶ Provide the class with some sentences about an aspect of the war. For example, *Each day we fought our battles well and went on to tell our tales back home to our families*. Challenge them to reorganise or rewrite the sentences to make rhyming lines.

▶ Provide collage materials for the children to recreate a scene showing poppies growing amongst the graves on a battlefield.

▶ Think of other important dates in the year, which are remembered as anniversaries, such as Eid, Easter, Chinese New Year.

Soldiers' letters   PAGE 63

These short extracts are based on the letters sent home by some of the soldiers in the First World War. Although a lot of letters sent home from the soldiers at the front during the war were censored, some managed to get through uncensored, including the first two on the sheet. It is from sources such as these that people began to learn the truth about conditions at the front.

Discussing the letters

▶ Look at the first letter. Who wrote this? What is a 'private'? Ask what we call a person who was there at the time. Explain that this is a very useful historical source because it gives us an *eyewitness account* of what it was like. This can make it a reliable version of the situation.

▶ Talk about the things that the first soldier is unhappy about, for example the lack of rest, the water in the trenches and so on.

▶ Ask the children what this soldier and his comrades have begun to realise about the war. How long does the officer think the war will go on? What do they think the war is going to be like?

▶ Discuss what the soldier means at the end, how he is imagining what the war is going to be like in the future.

▶ Look at the second letter. Ask the children why the soldiers have been getting out of their trenches. (For example, they had become tired of the war and of being stuck in the trenches. The German soldiers had also become tired of the war.)

▶ Look at the third letter. Ask what has happened in this account. What effect do the children think it has had on the writer?

▶ How do they think all the soldiers are beginning to feel about the war?

Activities

▶ Working individually or in pairs, the children could imagine they are soldiers in the First World War and write letters home to their families.

▶ Challenge the children to write newspaper reports using information from the letters.

▶ Organise the children into pairs and give each child the role of either interviewer or interviewee. Ask them to devise some short interviews of 'soldiers just back from the front'. Alternatively, adopt the role of a soldier yourself, and allow the children to ask you questions about the war.

▶ Research the story of the Christmas Day football match which was carried out between British and German soldiers in the First World War.

True or false?   PAGE 64

These simple sentences could be used in a number of ways. They might be useful as extension sheets for children who finish other work quickly. Alternatively, they could be used as assessment tasks by giving them to individuals to work on independently. Use them when you come towards the end of work on this topic.

Time word cards (1)

a very long time ago

a short time ago

now

then

recently

before

after

Time word cards (2)

first
second
century
decade
1918
1940s
1914

◣ SCHOLASTIC
PHOTOCOPIABLE

Commemoration word cards

commemorate

remembrance

anniversary

Cenotaph

veteran

wreath

two-minute silence

Specific events word cards

World War I

World War II

conflict

Armistice

ceasefire

SCHOLASTIC
PHOTOCOPIABLE

Evidence word cards

memorial

eyewitness

letter

firsthand

account

From left to right, by kind permission of Popperfoto, © Scholastic Ltd and © Doug Kneller.

First World War timeline

World War I ends

11th November 1918

John McCrae writes 'In Flanders Fields'

1915

World War I begins

1st August 1914

■ SCHOLASTIC
PHOTOCOPIABLE

Account of the First World War

In the summer of 1914, a very long time ago, a terrible war broke out between many of the countries of Europe, including Britain and Germany. The war came to be known as the Great War, later it was called the First World War.

This war broke out in the time of your great-great-grandparents. In those days, most people thought that war was a glorious thing. They wanted to fight to save their country. People on both sides felt the same. They did not know about the bad things that happened in war, because in those days there was no television and there were no photographs of wars for ordinary people to see.

Many young men rushed to join the army. They thought that they would quickly win. They thought the war would be over very soon. They were wrong because the war did not end for another four years. These young men also expected to have a good time and thought that it would be an exciting adventure. They soon found that this was wrong too. They were sent to France to face the enemy.

The soldiers had to live in trenches, where they could shelter from the gunfire. The trenches were deep and muddy. Many rats lived down in there too. The young men were often crouched in the mud, cold, wet and hungry, listening to the roaring guns of the enemy. Some young men became very ill, deafened or shocked by the terrible noise of bombs exploding nearby.

Often the order came that they must go 'over the top'. They called this 'OTT'. This meant that they had to run out over the top of their trenches to attack the enemy with their hand weapons. They had to fight with their pistols and bayonets. Of course, as soon as they came up out of their trenches many were killed by the gunfire.

After the war, people began to realise how many young men had died. They felt very sad and angry. They wanted to remember them and so they built, in every town and village, a special war memorial. They made statues or large crosses and put under them the names of all the soldiers, sailors and airmen from their town that had been killed.

Poppy Day began at the end of the war. The poem 'In Flanders Fields', written by a soldier in the war, told of poppies growing in the fields. It became so well known that the poppy became the symbol of remembrance. Poppy Day was first held on the 11th of November, 1921. The poppies were first made and sold in France in places that had been destroyed during the war.

In Flanders Fields

In Flanders Fields the poppies blow
Between the crosses, row on row,
That mark our place; and in the sky
The larks, still bravely singing, fly
Scarce heard amid the guns below.

We are the Dead. Short days ago
We lived, felt dawn, saw sunset glow,
Loved, and were loved, and now we lie
In Flanders fields.

Take up our quarrel with the foe:
To you from failing hands we throw
The torch; be yours to hold it high.
If ye break faith with us who die
We shall not sleep, though poppies grow
In Flanders fields.

Lieutenant Colonel John McCrae MD (1872–1918)

© Joy Monkhouse

Soldiers' letters

The soldiers in the trenches near the front line need more rest. We are having to live with the water which is over our knees most of the time. We all think that the war is going to last some time yet, not the few weeks we hoped. Our officer thinks it might be another twelve months before it is over. The war has only just begun and its going to be a terrible war. All the young lads at home being trained will take our places when we are killed. The sooner people understand this, the better.

We have just been able to come out of the trenches after being in there for six days. We have been up to our waists in water. While we were in the trenches, one of the Germans came over to our trench for a cigarette. He walked back again smoking it, and he was not fired at. We and the Germans all started walking about in the open between the two trenches, repairing them, and there was no firing at all. I think they are all getting fed up with it.

We started away just after dawn from our camp and I think it was about an hour later that we encountered the enemy. They were on the opposite side of the valley and as we came over the brow of the hill they opened on us with rifle fire and shrapnel from about 900 yards. We lost three officers and about 100 men killed and wounded in that half hour. I do not want any more days like that one.

SCHOLASTIC
PHOTOCOPIABLE

True or false?

▷ Read these sentences. Some are true and some are false. Write out the ones that you think are true.

Poppies are used to remember the people killed in the war.

The young men enjoyed the First World War.

The trenches were very warm and comfortable.

People were glad when the war ended.

Remembrance Day is held every year.

The names of the dead soldiers are written on the memorials.

TRANSPORT

Content, skills and concepts

This chapter on transport, although not specified within the exemplary materials in the QCA Scheme of Work for history at Key Stage 1 in England, may still be taught as a unit of work in its own right as an alternative to those suggested in the QCA scheme. It is also a suggested topic for the 'People in the past' part of the Scottish curriculum's social studies programme. The chapter will assist you in planning and resourcing a unit on cars, bicycles, aeroplanes and bridges. Together with the Transport Resource Gallery, this chapter provides materials to support the teaching of similarities and differences between transport today and in the past.

Oral history, discussion, and sorting and describing objects are all prior learning activities which will have introduced relevant skills and concepts to the children in younger age groups, before they progress to the skills and concepts in this unit. Suggestions for the further development of these skills form part of this chapter.

Resources on the CD-ROM

Photographs of cars, bicycles, aeroplanes and bridges from the past and the present are provided on the CD-ROM. Teacher's notes containing background information about these resources are included in this chapter as well as ideas for activities. There are also two video clips – one showing the old-fashioned, labour-intensive car-building process and one the more modern, automated process. The video clips, will involve the children with real-life experiences in both an accessible and engaging.

Photocopiables pages

Photocopiable resources are provided within the book and in PDF format on the CD from which they can be printed. They include:
▶ word cards which highlight the essential vocabulary of this topic
▶ a timeline
▶ accounts about journeys by car in 1890 and the present day.
Teacher's notes are provided in this chapter to accompany all the photocopiable pages.

The photocopiable pages are designed both to interest the children in the resources from the CD, and also to introduce them to notions of the past. They aim to enable children to make comparisons between different times in the past and also between the past and the present day.

History skills

Skills such as observing, describing, sorting, sequencing, comparing, inferring, listening, speaking, reading, writing and drawing are all involved in the activities provided. For example, children will observe closely the differences between the photographs of very old, 1950s and modern cars. They can learn to use descriptive vocabulary to talk about and compare the different cars. They will watch the video clips and perhaps be involved in discussing these and writing about them.

Historical understanding

In the course of the suggested tasks, a further aim is for children to begin to develop their notions of old and new, the past, the passing of time and of different periods in the past. They will also develop an awareness that in some ways things are different in the past, but in other ways the same. They will also begin to understand that there are different times in the past, and that these were also different from each other. Some of the more formal terminology related to chronology, such as *century*, is introduced in this chapter.

Photograph © Ingram Publishing

NOTES ON THE CD-ROM RESOURCES

An old car

This very early car from the late Victorian period (1890s) was one of the first cars built and seated only two people. The major differences between this early car and a modern one include the fact that it is almost completely open, has no steering wheel, and used solid tyres, like the bicycles of that time. This car is possibly powered by electricity; it wasn't until 1910 that using petrol to power cars became standard.

1950s car

In the 1950s, this car (a Standard Vignale Vanguard) was considered quite advanced, spacious and comfortable, and it conformed to the safety standards of the day. It seated four or five passengers and used leaded petrol, considered very environmentally unfriendly today.

Modern car

This Jaguar XKR Coupé is an example of a more expensive, luxury car. The car reaches high speeds easily and can take travellers great distances quickly, comfortably and safely.

Discussing the photographs
▶ Discuss all three pictures, comparing the cars and noting what the children can say about them.
▶ Ask the children if we see cars like these every day. Is there one kind of car we might see? Ask them to say which one. Ask why we do not see cars like the others around so much. (If the children are still unaware of the historical dimension you will need to draw their attention to features of the cars that indicate that they are old-fashioned.)
▶ Discuss how one car is new, or modern, one is old, and the third one is very old. Look at the details and talk about how we know this.

Activities
▶ Ask the children to sequence the three cars in time order. (They may begin with either the modern or the very old car.) Discuss how they have sequenced the images, and how there are two ways of doing this – forwards in time or backwards. (To make this activity more understandable for the very young, or less able children, provide them with a 'sorting board' divided into three boxes, into which they can sort their pictures.)
▶ Print out the three pictures and ask the children to write their own short captions below each one. Provide less able children with word cards (see photocopiable pages 72–3) to match to the pictures.
▶ Read 'A journey by car in 1890' (photocopiable page 79) and 'A modern car journey' (photocopiable page 78) to the children.
▶ Collect old and new model cars for the children to sort into sets according to age. (Discuss the difference between *old* meaning 'worn out' or meaning 'old-fashioned'.)
▶ Make a 'road through time' on the floor of the classroom and put onto it toy cars, in a sequence according to age. Discuss how this makes a line which can be drawn on paper to make a simple timeline.
▶ Watch the two videos 'Assembling the early car' and 'Modern car-building' and discuss the similarities and differences between them.

The penny-farthing

The penny-farthing was one of the earliest bicycles to be invented. The rider, usually a man, perched precariously above the large wheel and used pedals attached to its central hub. A second very small wheel was there merely to enable greater balance.

The name 'penny-farthing' is an interesting one, based on the coins of the period, when the penny was the largest of the copper coins and the farthing the smallest. If any examples of the coins could be made available, this would make the choice of name abundantly clear to the children.

1930s Raleigh bicycle

The 1930s Raleigh bicycle shown here was clearly a relatively new type. The all-steel frame probably made it considerably lighter and easier to handle than the old iron-framed bicycles which preceded it. This bicycle has been specially adapted to make it comfortable to ride and easy to mount for women wearing skirts. It is very different from the penny-farthing in that the wheels are almost the same size. There are a number of other design changes, which include the shape of the handle bars, the mudguards on the wheels and the bell.

Modern mountain bike

The mountain bike, by contrast, is designed for maximum strength, speed and security, with well-balanced wheels, a low centre of gravity for the rider, strong pneumatic tyres with a good grip, gears and many other safety features. As its name suggests, it was designed for off-road use, on tough terrain, which became a popular sport towards the end of the 20th century. The mountain bike gives the rider a much smoother, more comfortable, faster ride than both the penny-farthing with its solid rubber tyres and the 1930s bicycle.

Discussing the photographs

▶ Look at the picture of the penny-farthing and ask the children to guess what they think it is. What clues can they use to help them identify it? (For example, wheels, handlebars.) What other clues can they find to tell them that it is old? (The design, the dress of the rider.)

▶ See if volunteers can guess how long ago the penny-farthing was used. Help the children to place this picture on the class timeline.

▶ Introduce the class to its name, the 'penny-farthing'. Explain why the bicycle was so named if possible, showing them examples or pictures of the Victorian coins they were named after. Encourage the children to use new vocabulary during the discussion and ask them to read the word cards on photocopiable page 74.

▶ Look at the 1930s bicycle and discuss what changes have been made since the days of the penny-farthing. Talk about the all-steel feature.

▶ Who would be able to ride the 1930s bicycle? When could it be ridden? (For example, at any time, it is intended to be a casual activity.)

▶ Compare all three photographs and ask the children to notice things that are different and things that are the same.

▶ Looking at the 'Modern mountain bike', ask the class if they can work out why this is called a mountain bike. Ask: *Why are the children riding the mountain bikes wearing helmets?* Do the children think that the mountain bikes are fashionable? Discuss why. (For example, the goggles, the modern dress of the children, the chunky wheels.)

Activities

▶ Ask the children to sequence the three bicycles in time order. Discuss how they have sequenced the images, and how there are two ways of doing this – forwards in time or backwards. (See also a similar activity on cars, above.)

▶ Identify the children who have bikes at home, and which ones have mountain bikes. Work together to build a list of words which describe their bikes.

▶ In shared writing, write some sentences about why the children like to ride their bikes.

▶ Make a large wall timeline and ask for volunteers to place the pictures in their correct places. Discuss how they find the clues which enable them to do this. How do they know which picture is oldest?

▶ As part of a shared writing session, complete the similarities and differences chart, 'Old and new', on photocopiable page 80 about the penny-farthing and the mountain bike.

Farman aeroplane

This photograph, taken in 1909, of the Farman, or box-kite biplane, shows one of the most popular early aeroplanes, which was widely imitated. The machine was named after Henry Farman, of the Farman brothers, who had established themselves as leading aviators at the beginning of the 20th century. It ran on wheels, rose like a modern aeroplane and then came down again safely. Henry Farman himself went on to set numerous altitude and endurance records and made the first kilometre circuit in Europe.

Spitfire

The Spitfire is well known for its role in the aerial fighting during the Battle of Britain in World War II. A small and highly manoueverable aircraft, it was highly regarded by the airforcemen who flew in it and easily recognisable to the people on the ground, anxious to distinguish it from the aircraft used by the enemy. It was designed in 1936 by RJ Mitchell, and used a single propeller and Rolls-Royce Merlin engine. It was regarded by many as one of the best fighter aircraft of its day and is still respected for its elegant design.

Stealth bomber

Officially called the B-2 Spirit, this aeroplane was first publicly displayed in California in 1988. Its success in destroying enemy targets has been demonstrated in conflicts at the end of the 20th century during lengthy non-stop flights. It is capable of delivering conventional and nuclear weapons and represents a major technological breakthrough, in that it can bring massive firepower to bear in a short time, anywhere on the globe. It is known as the 'stealth' bomber because it is difficult to detect. Because of its wing design, special materials and coatings, it can penetrate the most sophisticated modern defences easily.

Discussing the photographs

▶ Compare the pictures of all three aeroplanes. What do the children notice about them? Why do they all look different? Where might they be able to see the older ones? (For example in old films.) Why is this? (Because they are out of use.)

▶ Discuss how one aeroplane is new, or modern, one is old, and the third one is very old. Look at the details and talk about how we can tell which is which.

▶ Tell the children some of the history and background information about the aeroplanes.

Activities

▶ Ask the children to sequence the three photographs in time order. (They may begin with either the modern or the very early aeroplane.) Discuss how they have sequenced the images, and how there are two ways of doing this – forwards in time or backwards.

▶ Organise the children to work in pairs with copies of the pictures and ask them to write their own short captions below each picture. Provide less able children with the word cards from photocopiable pages 72 and 75 to help them.

Tarr Steps

Tarr Steps is a medieval 'clapper' bridge over the River Barle, in Exmoor, Somerset. The steps span the river using large slabs of flat stone. There is no cement or mortar used to support the bridge or hold the construction together; the weight of the stones on their own has kept the bridge in place for hundreds of years. The bridge is an example of one of the simplest types of construction.

General Wade's Bridge

This is a photograph of General Wade's Bridge at Aberfeldy, Scotland. Built in the mid 18th century, it spans a greater height and distance than the Tarr Steps through the use of multiple arches, known for their strength. This five-arched bridge is nearly 400 feet in length,

The Skye Bridge

The bridge shown in this picture has connected the Isle of Skye to mainland Scotland since 1995, providing a permanent link between the two. It is one of the world's longest span cantilever bridges, built in probably one of the most rugged and challenging of environments.

Discussing the photographs

▶ Look at the photograph of Tarr Steps and discuss its particular features. What is it made of? How was it made? Is it modern? Was it difficult to make?

▶ Look at General Wade's Bridge. Ask the children why they think it has this name. Discuss the differences between this bridge and Tarr Steps.

▶ Finally, encourage the children to talk about the Skye Bridge – does it look old or new? How do they know? Explain that it is called a *cantilever* bridge and discuss what this means. (Piers reach out from either end, across the water, and are joined by another section in the middle.)

▶ What do they think the Skye Bridge is made from? (Reinforced concrete and steel.)

▶ Does the Skye Bridge look like it is a long bridge? How many arches and different parts can they see? Tell the class how this is now one of the longest bridges of its kind in the whole world. Find it on a recent map of Scotland.

Activities

▶ Help the children to find where these three bridges are on a large map of Britain. Find other bridges they have heard of. Discuss why the bridges were built in these places. Are there any bridges similar to the ones shown near the children's local area?

▶ Ask the children to work in pairs with the three pictures, to put them in order of when they think they were built. Ask each pair to tell the class what order they chose and why.

▶ Ask for volunteers to place the bridges on a timeline.

▶ Find other pictures of bridges, and place these on a timeline. Challenge the children to find as many bridges as they can. These could be displayed around the walls.

▶ Talk about why we need bridges and how we have learned to make bigger ones.

Video: assembling the early car

This silent video clip gives a brief glimpse into the car-building process when it was in its infancy, early in the last century (1913). Despite the fact that this appears to be a large and very busy factory, full of cars, people and machines, on closer inspection, it is possible to see that only quite small tasks are being completed. All the work on the cars is carried out by hand. The machines appear only to be used for making parts to put onto the cars. There are many cars standing waiting for parts to be fitted. Men are busy carrying things and fitting parts with hand-held small tools. In general, it is a very slow process.

This video clip (and the following one) is short, and children will benefit from looking at it a number of times. Watching the video will develop children's understanding of change and continuity, cause and effect, and the nature of historical sources.

Discussing the video clip

▶ Ask the children what they think is happening in this short video. What can they see? Where do they think it was filmed?

▶ Ask if it seems to be a present-day video clip, or one from the past. How do they know; what are the clues? (For example, the clothes and caps being worn; the style of the cars.)

▶ Discuss how the cars are being made. Ask if the children think the cars will be finished quickly or if it may take some time. Can they work out what the different stages of the process are? What do the children think the men are using the machines for?

Activities

▶ Help the children decide where this video would fit on a timeline. Review the language associated with this, for example *old-fashioned*, *long ago*, *almost a century ago*.

▶ Ask the children to describe the way the work is being done, introducing the term 'human labour' to them. Explain how, in the past, large numbers of people were needed to make things, whereas they are not today. Ask volunteers to explain why this is.

▶ Make a list of the jobs they have seen being done on the video.

▶ Compare this clip with 'Video: modern car-building' – for example, in the old car factory, more people worked at small jobs, while in the modern one, more machines are used.

Video: modern car-building

This video clip, with musical background, from the 1980s shows a modern car being made by robotic machines in a large car factory. What is distinctive about it is the almost total absence of any human labour at this point of the production process. Large car parts are moved and fitted together by machines, even the smaller parts being screwed or bolted. Although much of the finishing is done by hand, the major building work is carried out by robots, including painting the bodywork.

Discussing the video

▶ Ask the children what they can see in this video. What is happening here? Ask if they think it is a modern factory or an old-fashioned one. How do they know this?

▶ Do the children know what we call machines that work like this? Discuss all the things that the robots can do. Explain why robots are used in present-day factories.

▶ Ask the children to try to remember how many cars they saw being made at once. Ask how quickly these large jobs were being done.

▶ Discuss the costs of making cars by hand compared with making them by machine. Explain how this means that more people can afford to buy their own car.

Activities

▶ Help the children decide where this video would fit on a timeline. Review the language associated with this, for example *modern*, *recent*, *present day*.

▶ Challenge the children to describe the way the robots work, using as many descriptive terms as they can, for example *huge*, *giant*, *heavy*, *strong*, *quickly* and so on.

▶ Look at the photographs (provided on the CD) of 'Modern car', '1950s car' and 'An old car'. How do the children think these were built?

NOTES ON THE PHOTOCOPIABLE PAGES

Word cards PAGES 72–6

A number of specific types of vocabulary have been introduced on the word cards:

▶ words related to the passing of time and chronology, such as *older, newer, recent*

▶ words associated with cars, bicycles, aeroplanes and bridges, such as *engine, wheels, pedals, cockpit, arch*.

Encourage the children to think of other appropriate words to add to those provided, in order to build up a word bank for the theme of transport. They could also use the cards in displays, in matching activities and to help them in writing captions for their pictures. Once you have made copies of the word cards, cut them out and laminate them. Use them as often as possible when talking about transport or for word games.

Activities

▶ Add further vocabulary to the set of words, using any suggested by the children, such as words to do with travelling – *exciting, fast, far away, holidays* and so on.

▶ Make displays of different types of transport, and use the word cards to label them, for example *modern, old-fashioned, land transport, sea transport, air transport/travel*.

Cars timeline PAGE 77

This timeline introduces the idea of a sequence of objects in chronological order. It could be adapted for the classroom in the form of a long string stretched across the room, to represent the distance in time. The kind of timeline shown here can be useful at the end of the topic, for checking children's understanding of sequence and chronology.

Discussing the timeline

▶ At the beginning of the topic, ask the class what they think this timeline shows.

▶ Discuss what we mean by *Victorian*. What does *20th century* mean? Ask the children to give dates that are part of the 20th century. Discuss what *present* or *present day* mean.

▶ Talk about how the past in Victorian times is different compared with other times in the past, like the 1950s. Explain how different periods in the past are different from each other.

Activities

▶ Give each child a copy of a blank timeline and small pictures of cars at each period. Pictures can be printed from the CD and reduced in size. Ask the children to arrange the pictures in the correct order on their timeline, check that they are right and then paste them on.

▶ Add other periods to the timeline if the children have a good grasp of what they mean.

A modern car journey

PAGE 78

The content of this simple, non-fiction text on a journey in a modern car is probably familiar to most children and therefore enables them to identify with the subject. It aims to contrast sharply with the following account about a journey in an early car, to show the kind of developments which have taken place over the last century. The account will be useful as a stimulus for discussion, as an aid for children's own recollections and as a stimulus for children's own writing about their experiences of car journeys.

Discussing the text

▶ Read and re-read the text during a whole class shared reading session. Ask if any of the children have had experiences like this. Have they made long journeys by car? Where have they been on these journeys? Discuss how they felt during the journey. Ask what sort of things they did during the trip. Find out what they liked/did not like about it.

▶ Ask how they think it compares with a journey in an old-fashioned car. What would they have liked/disliked about a journey long ago?

▶ Ask if anyone has seen a very modern car with many dials and controls. Have they heard computers in these cars giving instructions to the drivers and passengers?

Activities

▶ Invite the children to collect and bring to school any pictures they can find of modern cars. Make a wall display of them.

▶ Devise a short play about a car journey and work with the children during a shared writing session to write a simple script.

▶ Compare this text with 'A journey by car in 1890' on photocopiable page 79. Do the children like the old or new car better? Discuss what features they like.

A journey by car in 1890

PAGE 79

This explanatory account gives details of early cars and the kind of experiences that passengers are likely to have had. At the time, the speed of these cars was very limited, compared with what is expected today. Consequently, drives of any significance would have been long, and you would not have expected to go very far. Exposed to the elements and rough roads, people would have found a journey by car at this time quite tiring.

Discussing the text

▶ Read and re-read the text during a whole-class shared reading session. Establish how long ago people would have driven in cars like this.

▶ Ask for volunteers to find from the text all the things that would have made a journey uncomfortable. What other reasons were there for a car journey feeling rather uncomfortable? (For example, the roads, the lack of services for motorists.)

▶ Together, make a list of the various things people would have had to wear if they were going out for the day in a car like this.

Activities

▶ Collect other pictures of veteran and vintage cars. Help the children to place them correctly on the class timeline.

▶ During shared writing, compose a short story about a car journey in the year 1890.

▶ Compare this text with 'A modern car journey' on photocopiable page 78. Do the children like the old or new car better? Discuss what features they prefer.

Old and new

PAGE 80

This table could be used at the end of the topic to compare the photographs provided in the Transport Resource Gallery on the CD. Specify to the children whether they are comparing cars, bicycles, aeroplanes or bridges. The children will have already looked at relevant pictures and photographs and will have made suggestions themselves. Model writing the similarities and differences on the board as the discussion takes place. The creation of a word bank will have helped the children become familiar with the vocabulary they will need to use in completing the table.

recent

modern

older

oldest

newer

newest

Car word cards

wheels
horn
seats
starting handle
steering wheel
headlight
door
mirror

Bicycle word cards

pedal
saddle
wheel
brakes
gears
cyclist
helmet
goggles

Aeroplane word cards

wings
tail
engine
wood
fabric
metal
cockpit
propeller

Bridges word cards

arch

arched

span

cantilever

stone

metal

concrete

river

From left to right, © Topham Picture Point © British Motor Industry Heritage Trust and image of XKR Coupé kindly supplied by Jaguar Cars Ltd.

Cars timeline

present day

20th century

Victorian times

A modern car journey

In the 21st century, cars are expected to have many features that were not even dreamed about 50 years ago. They are built for comfort and safety, and have to be designed to look fashionable. They are made very quickly, using robots in large car-making factories. Cars must have comfortable seating, suitable tyres and features such as anti-roll mechanisms to produce a safe, smooth and comfortable ride. They can travel very fast, on specially designed roads, such as motorways. A long journey to a different part of the country is now expected only to take a few hours, and many people travel great distances every day to work.

A modern car journey could take you across the country in a few hours. The car can travel at speeds higher than seventy miles an hour. Although it goes so fast, the journey is very quiet inside the car. Usually, people listen to the radio or to a CD or tape while they are in their cars. They can travel wearing any type of clothing they wish, since the temperature is controlled inside the car. The passengers are protected from the weather and the air-conditioning or heating can make the inside of the car just as comfortable as being inside a house. In some cars, the driver can be told the outside temperature, whether the doors are closed, and if there is any kind of problem with the car. All these facilities are controlled by a computer chip connected to the engine.

Every so often on a motorway, there are cafés and places to stop and eat. These service stations have all kinds of facilities, including amusements for children and shops. If anyone thinks there is a problem with their car, there are many different people that can be called out to help, such as the Automobile Association, or the Royal Automobile Club. You are likely to arrive at your destination feeling relaxed and comfortable in comparison with the experiences of people travelling by car 100 years ago. One change which has not been so welcome, of course, is the modern problem of traffic jams, which can slow down or stop your car for many hours.

A car journey in 1890

The new 'horseless carriage', or motor car, was soon very popular in Victorian England. It could only be bought by fairly rich people at that time, but it gave much enjoyment to those who could afford it. The first cars were open topped, so a journey in one of these was quite cold and windy. To go out for a ride, you would need hat, gloves, scarves and warm clothes, even in the summer. Ladies would tie scarves round their heads to keep their hats on during the drive. Such car journeys would also be fairly eventful, since many things used to go wrong with the cars. They were always breaking down.

The journey would have been quite slow, because the car did not go much faster than ten or twelve miles an hour. Anyway, people were afraid to go much faster than this. They thought it far too dangerous. So a trip out into the countryside from the town would take most of the day. You would have to set off early in the morning to have enough time to get there safely, and you would not return till the end of the day.

The trip was very bumpy. The wheels on these early cars were solid and did not pass smoothly over any uneven roads. They caused the car to jolt and bump as it went along. The seats were hard too. As well as this, the roads were not specially made for car journeys. Most people still used horses or horses and carriages or carts, and uneven roads were the norm. As you can imagine, when they got back from a car journey in a car like this early model, people would have felt quite tired, cold and uncomfortable.

Old and new

▷ Make lists of the things that are the same and different about the pictures your teacher has given you.

Things that are the same	Things that are different

■SCHOLASTIC
PHOTOCOPIABLE